THE SCREEN GREATS

Clint EASTWOOD

THE SCREEN GREATS

Clint EASTWOOD

ALAN FRANK

Exeter Books

NEW YORK

Photographic acknowledgments

Camera Press, London 62; Frank Driggs Collection, New York 13, 26; Flashbacks, London 8, 30 bottom, 48 bottom, 54, 63, 64 bottom, 67, 69, 77; Keystone Press Agency, London 21, 42 bottom, 68; Kobal Collection, London 2, 16 top, 16 bottom, 17, 18, 19, 23, 24, 25, 27, 28, 29, 31, 32 top, 33 bottom, 34 top, 36, 37, 38, 39 top, 42 top, 43, 45, 48 top, 49, 50, 51, 52, 53, 55, 56, 57, 58, 59, 61, 64 top, 65, 66, 70, 75; National Film Archive, London 34 bottom, 44, 79; Popperfoto, London 20, 33 top, 35, 40, 41; Rex Features, London 7, 9, 11, 12, 14, 32 bottom, 39 bottom, 46, 47, 60, 72, 73, 74, 76, 78; Syndication International, London 30 top, 71.

Front cover. *Joe Kidd* (Universal/Malpaso). Kobal Collection.
Back cover. *Dirty Harry* (Warner Bros.). Kobal Collection.
Frontispiece. *Two Mules for Sister Sara* (Universal). Kobal Collection.

Copyright © 1982 The Hamlyn Publishing Group Limited
First published in the USA in 1982
by Exeter Books
Exeter is a trademark of Simon & Schuster
Distributed by Bookthrift
Bookthrift is a registered trademark of Simon & Schuster
New York, New York

For copyright reasons this edition is only for sale
within the USA

All rights reserved. No part of this publication may be
reproduced, stored in a retrieval system, or transmitted,
in any form or by any means, electronic, mechanical,
photocopying, recording or otherwise, without the permission
of The Hamlyn Publishing Group Limited, Astronaut House,
Feltham, Middlesex, England.

ISBN 0-89673-135-9
Printed in Italy

CONTENTS

THE BEGINNINGS OF THE LONER 6

A FALSE START IN HOLLYWOOD 15

RAWHIDE AND SPAGHETTI WESTERNS 21

THE ONE EXPRESSION OF STARDOM 29

DIRECTING, GOTHIC HUMOUR AND VIOLENCE 41

THE RETURN OF THE LONE STRANGER 52

STAR, ACTOR AND DIRECTOR 63

FILMOGRAPHY 80

THE BEGINNINGS OF THE LONER

Screen performers can, as a generalization, be divided into two major categories – stars and actors – and, more often than not, the two are by no means the same thing at all. Actors tend to be performers who, by their skill and talents are both critically recognized and appreciated by film makers who employ them in order to provide a solid backbone to movies designed to be a showcase for their stars. As such, then, the presence of actors *per se* in a movie may be acknowledged with pleasure by movie audiences but their inclusion in a film is usually not enough in itself to ensure that people will want to see the film. If there is one single characteristic which distinguishes the actor from the star, it is the unique quality of charisma, an intangible something, largely impossible to manufacture, which breaks away from the confines of the cinema screen to touch a special chord in the viewer, setting the star apart from the general run of movie performers. If an actor does not possess that charisma, he or she is highly unlikely to make the step from actor to star. And, as the history of the cinema shows only too well, there are performers who, despite all the hyperbole of studio publicity, the careful choice of screen vehicles and sometimes what appears in retrospect to be a misjudged and over-optimistic determination to create a star, failed to make that vital transition. By and large, film makers and studios do not make stars: that is the prerogative of the filmgoer, the person who really matters in the cinema since he or she is the final arbiter of screen success. Adolph Zukor, the great film pioneer, was right in the final analysis when he stated the (self-evident) dictum that the public is always right.

Of course, being an actor and being a star are far from being mutually exclusive. There have been stars whose early careers showed no signs that they were destined to become actors or that stardom was in store for them. In the heyday of the Hollywood studios, there was always a better than average chance that someone the studio top brass believed had the chance to become a star would ultimately make it. The output of movies was high and actors and, in particular players who appeared to have the potential for stardom, were given an opportunity to learn their craft in film after film until, hopefully, they clicked with the cinema-going public and made the hoped-for transition to stardom. Hollywood was a factory and the performers were part of that factory, part of the studios' property whose value needed to be maximized. But, with the collapse of the studio system, and the growth of the great enemy television, the chances for potential stars to be nurtured through film after film vanished: performers either became stars or remained in the ranks of supporting players – or even disappeared completely. Since the collapse of the great studios, there have been plenty of people who have starred in films: but they soon discovered that starring in a picture did not automatically make them a star, and the last two decades of movies are littered with performers whose much-heralded screen appearances failed to make the hoped-for impact with audiences, leaving the hunt for new stars, who would be, in the modern movie parlance, 'bankable', to continue.

A reasonable definition of stardom, then, is that which makes a player whom audiences world-wide will willingly pay their money to see and not care overmuch about the film in which he or she is appearing. Today there are precious few screen performers to whom that definition applies. Clint Eastwood, however, is most definitely in this category. The international success of his movies triumphantly proves this. And, despite popular belief, his stardom does not rely simply on the fact that an Eastwood film unfailingly depicts the same character. His career impressively proves that he is an actor of considerable range and abilities, with a sometimes uncanny skill at being able to predict just what cinema-goers want to see, a factor that is perhaps one of the most important and valuable requirements for screen success.

Even more importantly, Eastwood is not just a star. He is an actor whose technique, while apparently simple to the point of being

near invisible, makes him one of the finest working in the current cinema. His stardom goes back to the great traditions of the American anti-hero, best exemplified perhaps by Humphrey Bogart, and the small but unique band of actors who can dominate the screen simply by being on it, most perfectly exemplified by Gary Cooper. Indeed, Italian director-actor Vittorio de Sica, who made the episode *Un Sera Come Le Altre (A Night Like Any Other)* of the five-part movie *Le Streghe (The Witches)* (1967) with Eastwood, proclaimed him as: 'Absolutely the new Gary Cooper'.

Eastwood is more than simply a new Gary Cooper. While he shares Cooper's ability to focus all the attention on himself in a scene in which, apparently, he does nothing except stand in front of the camera, he is able to demonstrate, time after time, an acting skill in a variety of roles that even Cooper was unable to match. He has also shown himself to be a producer with a near-uncanny ability to find the right vehicle totally to match audience needs, as well as proving to be one of the finest film directors currently working. All too often, Eastwood's films have been critically commented upon in terms of their directors, especially those concerning Don Siegel, by those critics determined to espouse the fashionable *auteur* theory to the exclusion of all other factors contributing to a film's success. This is a dangerous point of view since it can all too easily lead to a dismissal of the major contribution of the star. The audiences who have confirmed Eastwood's stardom go to see Clint Eastwood films, not the films of particular directors, however fashionable they may be. The *auteur* theory, with the notable exceptions of Cecil B. De Mille and Alfred Hitchcock, belongs within the province of film critics and movie buffs and not to the people who really matter at the movies – those who actually pay to see films.

Eastwood, then, is a major star. That stardom is compounded of his charismatic persona, his ability as an actor, producer and director and perhaps above all, by his skill at knowing just what it is that the paying customer wants from a movie. He once defined it in a way that is difficult to refute when he said: 'A guy sits alone in a theatre. He's young and he's scared. He doesn't know what he's going to do with his life. He wishes he could be self-sufficient, like the man he sees up there on the screen, somebody who can look out for himself, solve his own problems. I do the kind of roles I'd like to see if I were still digging swimming pools

Star quality is difficult to define, but undoubtedly Eastwood has it. During ex-President Ford's golf tournament in Vail, Colorado, in 1978, with girl friend Sondra Locke as his golf-cart passenger, he draws the attention of all the female spectators.

Far right: The young Eastwood was not lacking in charm, but his immediate appeal would be as a clean-cut, athletic type, rather than the silent, menacing killer that brought him fame.

Below: The most dangerous man who ever lived. Certainly *A Fistful of Dollars* (United Artists) *was* the first motion picture of its kind, and the first which brought Eastwood universal success.

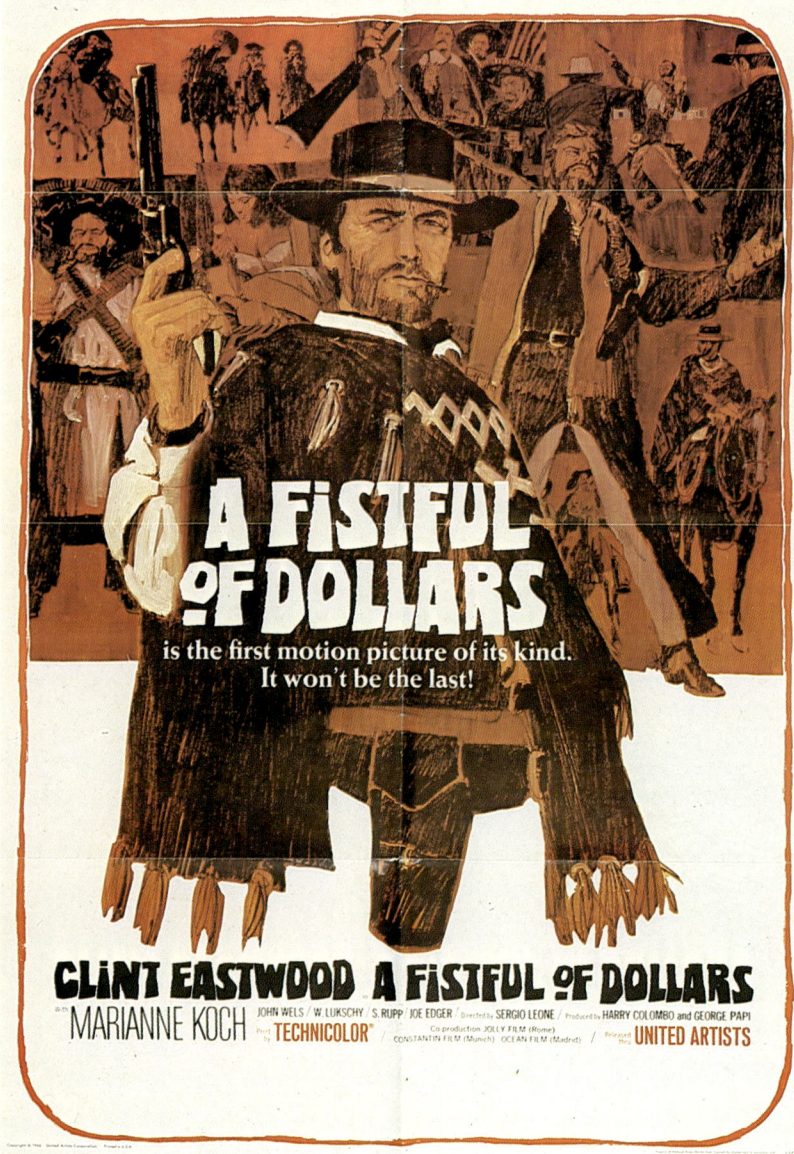

and wanted to escape my problems.'

Eastwood has come a long way since the days when he made a precarious living digging swimming pools. And, in the process, he has become an exemplar for cinema-goers all over the world, a superstar and a self-made millionaire. Almost uniquely, he has become a man whose name on a film is enough to guarantee its success.

Clint Eastwood was a child of the great American Depression, born in San Francisco on 31 May 1931. For those who believe in star signs, that makes him a Gemini, along with such screen luminaries as John Wayne, Laurence Olivier, Bob Hope, Judy Garland, Marilyn Monroe and Errol Flynn.

Be that as it may, his early days were hardly auspicious. His father, Clinton Eastwood Senior, after whom he was named, had, like so many Americans during the hard days of the 1930s, to travel around the country in search of whatever work there was. Jobs were difficult to find and even harder to keep and Eastwood Senior worked variously as an accountant and even a filling station attendant. The family lived in something like a dozen towns in northern California during Eastwood's childhood.

Given this nomadic style of upbringing, it was hardly surprising that the young Eastwood would grow up to be something of a loner and in many ways similar to the kind of characters he was later to play on the screen. By the time the Eastwoods came to live in Oakland, he had attended something like ten schools in as many years and had had to learn to be self-sufficient. He was quoted as saying: 'When you're a new kid in town, you always have to punch it out with the other kids the first day or so. Kids always seem to pick on tall kids too, and I was six feet (1.83m) tall at the age of 13.'

His character was formed early on in life and, getting along well with his parents, he came to subscribe to his father's philosophy that you don't get anything for nothing. He might go on to become something of a rebel but he would always go along with that particular aphorism, something that would hold him in good stead in his future life and career.

However, after a peripatetic early life that had taken him to Redding, Seattle, Sacramento, Spokane and Pacific Palisades, Eastwood settled at last when his father obtained employment with the Container Corporation of America in Oakland and Eastwood was able to start putting down roots.

He enrolled at Oakland Technical High School and began to make friends from whom he would not have to be parted when the family had to move on to the next town. Those nomadic days were over.

By the time he was 15, he was some six feet four inches (1.93m) in height and, having been initiated on his travels by his father into sport and the physical life, he was a natural for high school athletics, something that was to feature largely in later rosy biographies put out by Hollywood publicists. But, as he told various subsequent interviewers, he had an inherent shyness about putting himself forward into anything with a full-hearted enthusiasm. He stated that he was naturally an introvert and worried about making an exhibition of himself in public. Nonetheless, he became a first-rate basketball player at school and later claimed that his schooldays were among the happiest days of his life.

Incredibly, for someone who would become a screen idol, he found his introversion a distinct drawback when it came to girls. His shyness made the simple act of asking for a date a nightmare and, when he managed to pluck up the courage to ask for one, the experience was, more often than not, far from a happy one. He found that either he talked too much or was too taciturn, and it was finally through the efforts of his English teacher, Miss Jones, that he succeeded in breaking his generally introvert nature and releasing himself from the constraints of his tongue-tied shyness.

Miss Jones selected for one year's class project a play about a rebel youth. And, percipiently, she cast Eastwood in the role of the loner, persuading him to take the part. Eastwood hated the experience, and only the fact that his parents were looking forward to seeing him on stage kept him from quitting the play. He and his friend Harry Pendleton, who was playing his father in the production, met at the local drug store the night before the performance and agreed to give the play a miss. But, the following morning, they recanted and both appeared on stage. The experience, discovering that it was possible to lose himself in a fictional character whose attributes need not necessarily match his own inherent character, proved to be just what Eastwood needed to come to terms with his introversion. He was now 15 and it was then, he later recalled, that he grew up.

Eastwood's teenage days were much in the mould of normal American youngsters. He and his pals would go drag racing, and hang around local swimming pools (his father had taught him to be an excellent swimmer) and he became a good pianist and trumpet player and had a series of vacation jobs that included fire fighting in northern California and baling hay.

When he came to leave school, graduating in 1948, Eastwood had no clear idea what he wanted to do with his life. He had been something of a daydreamer at school and if he had any career ambition, it was to do a job that involved physical effort. About the one career idea that had never occurred to him was to become an actor. His experience in the class play for Miss Jones had been far too traumatic for that.

His first job after graduation was as a lumberjack in a timber mill on the Willamette River in Oregon. The work was tough, backbreaking physical labour but Eastwood enjoyed it, wanting to be alone and to earn his own way. He worked felling trees for a year, wanting nothing more in the evenings than to crash out on his bunk and sleep, and spending weekends with his fellow workers whooping it up in nearby Eugene.

However, America had now entered the Korean War and Eastwood realized that it would not be long before he received his call-up papers. So, about a month before his call-up was due, he quit Oregon and went to San Francisco where he did a variety of odd jobs and enjoyed himself waiting for his army service.

He was duly conscripted into the Army and sent up to Fort Ord, on the Monterey Peninsula, for induction and six weeks of tough basic training. He intended to make use of his time in the army to learn a skill and went to see the captain in charge of the Division Faculty classes. After telling the officer of the various jobs he had had since leaving school, Eastwood was asked if he could swim. On learning that he could, Eastwood was immediately assigned to be a swimming instructor at Fort Ord, joining a lieutenant and four sergeants who were already in charge of the Olympic-size swimming pool.

His military service could hardly have been bettered. He was able to move out of the barracks and live in one of the small dormitories that were attached to the pool and army life was far more like civilian life for him. He was very much his own boss, as long as he did not get into trouble and did his job properly and, finding that the $76 a month he was being paid was not enough, Eastwood was able to moonlight at nights, taking a job for four months at the Spreckles Sugar Company in Salinas Valley. But the combination of his daytime work and heavy physical labour at nights began to tell on him and finally Eastwood quit the sugar company and worked instead at the junior non-commissioned officer's club, conveniently situated a minute or so's walk from the swimming pool.

By this time Eastwood's parents had moved to Seattle and, while he was visiting them on a furlough, he had met a girl called Jean. Later, wanting to visit her again and to see his parents, an army buddy told him that it was possible to get from Fort Ord to Seattle and back on a weekend pass – and that it would not cost him anything.

The method was a simple one. It was explained to Eastwood that if he turned up at the Monterey Naval Air Station in uniform, he could be flown anywhere, as long as there was a spare seat on the aircraft. Duly Eastwood turned up at Monterey and was lucky, hitching a ride in a reconnaissance plane that was headed for Seattle. He had an enjoyable couple of days with Jean and his parents and then arrived back at the air base to find himself a flight back to Monterey.

There he ran into trouble. There were no planes due to return to Monterey and East-

Eastwood as a superstar is reticent about his private life, but his children are welcome on the film set. Here he rescues an airplane for his son Kyle. Aircraft trouble might have cost Eastwood his life in his army days.

wood had no money for a commercial ticket back to base. He had terrible visions of being posted AWOL and so he tried asking every pilot at the base.

Finally, his luck changed. He found a naval torpedo bomber that was due to fly back to San Francisco. But there was a problem, a big one.

There were no seats on the aircraft. Eastwood's powers of persuasion finally prevailed, however, and he took off for base crammed into a small compartment in the rear of the aircraft which was designed as a maintenance area and certainly not for carrying passengers.

Everything that could possibly go wrong did. Just after take-off, the door of the compartment sprang open at 6,000 feet (1,800m) and Eastwood found himself hanging on for dear life – and he discovered that the intercom connecting him to the pilot was not working. Eastwood was unable to make contact, although the pilot could hear him and was shouting at him that the door was open – not that Eastwood needed telling. Eastwood succeeded in pulling out a cable and looping it around the handle of the open door which more or less kept it shut.

Worse was still to come. As the aircraft continued to climb, Eastwood discovered that his oxygen mask was not working either and the pilot was unable to hear him when Eastwood spoke of his plight over the intercom. Eastwood finally blacked out. When he recovered consciousness, the aircraft was over Point Reyes – and about to crash into the sea. There was a dense fog enveloping the plane which was dangerously low on fuel.

When the plane hit the sea, Eastwood scrambled out of the maintenance compartment and made his way onto the wing, joining the pilot who had escaped from the cockpit. Not surprisingly, they decided to swim for the shore and to try to stick together in the water. But there was a heavy swell and the two were soon separated.

The swim back to shore was a nightmare, even for a powerful swimmer like Eastwood. It took him an hour before he could see the shore, but between him and the rocks was an eerie shoal of phosphorescent jelly fish.

Never share scenes with animals. It would be pleasant to record this picture as an early example of Eastwood getting to know one of his co-stars in a projected career as a cowboy, but it is merely Eastwood fooling about.

Eastwood in *For a Few Dollars More* (United Artists), his second starring part. This is the face of The Man with No Name.

Given the choice of drowning or being stung to death, Eastwood did not hesitate but swam through the jelly fish, finally making it to safety on the shore where once again he lost consciousness.

When he came too, he searched for his fellow survivor, but failed to locate him and then walked barefoot along the beach for some eight miles before finding a radio communications relay station. Later he was to say that he had not minded the swim but that the five-mile hike he had taken before finding a highway had been the part of his ordeal that had really bothered him.

Afterwards he discovered that the pilot had survived and had in fact hit the beach some 500 yards (450m) from where Eastwood landed. They had missed each other when Eastwood headed north while the pilot had gone south, landing up on a farm.

During his time at Fort Ord, Eastwood had met an assistant director with a film unit that Universal-International had sent to the camp to carry out location shooting. The assistant, impressed by the six foot four inch (1.93m) soldier had called him to the attention of the unit's director, who asked Eastwood to read a scene for him; despite his none-too-happy memories of his one and only attempt at acting at High School, Eastwood duly obliged. Things were different now and the director suggested to Eastwood that he get in touch with him at Universal when he completed his stint in the army.

It was during his army service that Eastwood – now well over his teenage shyness with girls – met Maggie Johnson. One of his friends, Don, was going out with a student at the University at California at Berkeley and suggested that Eastwood go along with him one weekend on a double date.

Eastwood agreed, and, at Berkeley, met Maggie Johnson, his blind date for the evening and also a university student. There was an immediate empathy between the two and Eastwood was later to say that he and Maggie had hit it off right away. 'She is', he went on to say, 'the kind of girl I really like. There's nothing phony about her. She has natural good looks. She's blonde and fairly tall for a woman, five feet seven (1.70m). I liked Maggie's sense of humour. And she's sure needed that good humour around me from time to time.'

After that first meeting, Eastwood and Maggie saw a great deal of each other at weekends and, when he finished his stint in the army, he decided to go to Los Angeles and enrol at the Los Angeles City College under a GI grant. He found an apartment in a block in Beverly Hills, paying his rent by working for the owners and, while he was at college, he worked variously as a filling station attendant, as a life guard and digging swimming pools. And he continued to court Maggie. The two of them would spend weekends at Newport Beach swimming, dancing and having barbecues with a like-minded crowd of friends and they went to jazz concerts and found that they shared a mutual interest in classical music, books, films and plays.

Eastwood and Maggie married during his Christmas vacation from Los Angeles City College on 19 December 1953 and she went on working for an export company while Eastwood continued his studies. But Eastwood was still unsure just what he wanted to do after he completed his studies. That was soon to change.

Eastwood married his wife Maggie during a Christmas vacation from college. In this picture they are at a party at the Directors Guild Theater in Hollywood to celebrate John Wayne's 200th picture, *True Grit*, in 1969.

A FALSE START IN HOLLYWOOD

Eastwood had never pursued with much effort the idea of becoming an actor, despite his friendship with would-be actors David Janssen and Martin Milner and his brief brush with film making while at Fort Ord. He had gone to Universal on his discharge from the army to try to see the director who had suggested that they should get in touch with each other when Eastwood had completed his military service, only to discover that the man was no longer with the studio. So Eastwood had enrolled at the Los Angeles City College and begun to study Business Administration, temporarily forgetting the idea of a screen career.

However, after his marriage, friends suggested that he have another go at Universal and, after he had spent a day at the studio watching filming, he found director Arthur Lubin had been persuaded to give him a screen test.

The test was a silent one, where he was required to stand and walk in front of the camera and later Eastwood was to say that the experience had scared him to death. Years afterwards he was to tell *Playboy* magazine that: 'I thought I was an absolute clod. It looked pretty good, it was photographed well, but I thought, "If that's acting, I'm in trouble".'

As usual, following the test, Eastwood had been told not to call the studio, that they would call him in due course. During the ensuing days he attempted to ring Lubin but failed to get through to him or have him return his calls.

It was not until nearly three weeks after making the test that Eastwood was woken up by a Universal Casting Director to be told that he was to be offered a stock acting contract with the studio at the princely sum of $75 a week, guaranteeing him 40 weeks work a year.

The money looked really good when compared with the $100 a month that Eastwood was receiving from his GI grant and he and Maggie were quite naturally elated at his sudden good fortune.

But, in the 1950s, the Golden Age of Hollywood – and of movie-going – was rapidly coming to an end. During the war audiences had been hungry for film entertainment and the cinemas had been packed, no matter what film was showing. With the end of the war, however, and faced with the harsh realities of having to make a peace-time living once more and with less time for the sort of escapism that the cinema could provide, people began to go to the pictures in ever-decreasing numbers. And now the electronic monster that would finally spell the end to the halcyon times of the cinema was beginning to invade the living rooms of American homes. Television, described by comedian Ernie Kovacs as: 'A medium, so called because it is neither rare nor well done', and 'Chewing gum for the eyes' by Frank Lloyd Wright, captured the viewing habits of the nation. Quality did not really matter: what was important was that the television set was there and entertainment, good, bad or simply indifferent was now available at the turn of a switch, without cost or the bother of going out to a cinema. Movie pioneer Samuel Goldwyn accurately summed up its appeal, and defined its lethal potential as far as pictures were concerned when he said: 'Why should people go out and pay money to see bad films when they can stay at home and see bad television for nothing?'

The major studios felt the pinch as people stayed at home and watched television. True, there were still relatively lucrative overseas markets for films in countries where television had yet to gain a stranglehold on potential movie audiences, but the United States had always been the most valuable market and no studio could survive on overseas markets without a profitable home market to sustain their output. The days of 'anything goes' were over and, until the major film studios finally capitulated, first by selling their libraries of old films to television and then, in particular in the case of Universal, going into television production themselves, movies were having to fight for their existence against near-insurmountable odds.

When Eastwood began his career as a Universal stock contract player, the chances of the sort of careful star build up that had

15

Above: Universal-International's Talent School. Under the eye of drama coach Jack Kosslyn (left), Eastwood and Gia Scala play a scene for fellow class members.

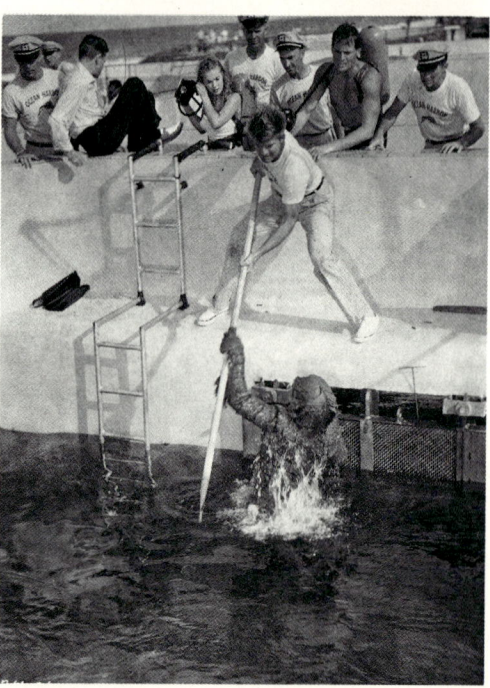

Right: Eastwood can be seen (top left) playing what is a very minor role in his first film, *Revenge of the Creature* (Universal-International). The stars John Agar (with aqualung) and Lori Nelson look on with mild horror.

existed in the 1930s and 1940s were almost non-existent. There simply was neither the time nor the money. Fortunately for him, however, Universal was busier than most studios, making unambitious programme films which succeeded in getting healthy cinema exposure, albeit usually in unremarkable double bills.

However, if Eastwood's career at Universal could hardly be described as a starry one, it did serve to give him a solid and valuable grounding in the art and craft of being a movie actor. He became a member of Universal's Talent School and learned to ride, fence and even to dance, and he was able to attend drama school in the studio, supplementing those classes with evening work with an outside group. Slowly, he began to get the opportunities to apply some of what he was learning in front of the cameras.

On many of his early films, he worked in bits so small, sometimes simply as an off-screen voice or as a near supernumary, that these minor appearances passed without mention and he was unbilled.

His accredited screen debut came in a horror movie, *Revenge of the Creature* (1955) directed by Jack Arnold and a sequel to his highly successful *Creature from the Black Lagoon*, made in 3D in 1954. The movie was very much the mixture as before with the Creature, brought back from its Amazon home to Florida, breaking out of captivity in a large exhibition tank to wreak traditional monster havoc until the last reel. The stars were John Agar and Lori Nelson, and Eastwood was cast as a laboratory assistant named Jennings whose contribution to the movie consisted of one scene in which, dressed in a white laboratory coat, he discovered a white mouse in his pocket. Although Arnold was later to be recognized as one of the major film makers in the science fiction and horror movie field, *Revenge of the Creature* was greeted in the *Monthly Film Bulletin* with: 'This naive and indifferently played shocker . . .', and even the fact that it was filmed in 3D did little to encourage contemporary critics. Eastwood himself went unnoticed at the time. As always, long after the event, critics discovered him in the film when it was re-shown in Britain in 1980, the *Sunday Mirror* commenting: 'If you are quick you may spot Clint Eastwood in his first three-line screen role as a laboratory technician', and the *Daily Mail* reviewer said: 'Incidentally, the film gives the lie to the notion that you can always spot a potential superstar in an unrewarding role. There's a chap with a Tony Curtis hair-cut who plays an inefficient laboratory assistant. He's neglected to feed the cat in the cage – or was it the rat? I've forgotten. I'd have forgotten the actor, too, who doesn't even rate a mention in the credits. His name, for the record, was Clint Eastwood.'

Not even the most percipient star spotter could have seen in Eastwood's part in *Revenge of the Creature* or his next, *Tarantula* (1955) any intimations of the star to be. Again for director Jack Arnold, Eastwood played a bit as a jet pilot who bombed the giant spider in *Tarantula* with napalm at the climax of the movie. The film itself was an impressive and tense addition to the 1950s monster movie cycle but Eastwood's brief appearance, effectively hidden behind a

flying helmet, mask and goggles in the cockpit of the jet aircraft, was hardly likely to do anything for him and his career.

Next came an equally unmemorable appearance in *Lady Godiva* (GB: *Lady Godiva of Coventry*), directed by Arthur Lubin, who had been in charge of Eastwood's initial screen test at Universal. It would be pleasant to be able to record that, with memories of the test in mind, Lubin had instantly been able to spot Eastwood's star potential but that was far from the case. *Lady Godiva* was simply a studio assignment for Eastwood, crediting him as 'First Saxon', and the film itself earned from *Monthly Film Bulletin* the comment: '. . . an unevenly sustained costume piece; flashes of humour, though making for a comic strip atmosphere, at least ensure that some episodes go with a swing, but in its most seriously intentioned moments it borders on dullness.' Which, to be fair to Universal, was hardly a surprise in the 1950s where the full potential (such as there was) of Lady Godiva's naked ride through Coventry could hardly be fulfilled given the current censorship restrictions.

His next picture, however, *Francis in the Navy* (1955), the latest in the series of farcical

Without his growth of beard and the other trappings of the cold ruthless character he frequently played, Eastwood has the kind of looks that in another age might have seen him reach the top in vastly different roles.

A young, clean-shaven Eastwood (right) confronting Maureen O'Hara, the star of one of the films of his 'apprenticeship' with Universal-International, *Lady Godiva* (GB: *Lady Godiva of Coventry*).

fantasies starring Donald O'Connor and a talking mule (voiced by Chill Wills) united Eastwood with his friend David Janssen and this time gave him sufficient screen time as 'Jonesy' to be critically noticed and variously referred to by film critics as 'handsome', 'promising' or 'engaging'. The role, however, was a small one, and playing support to a talking ass was hardly likely to be of much help in advancing anybody's career.

This was followed by an uncredited and minute part in *Away All Boats* (1956) which starred George Nader, who had been the leading man in *Lady Godiva*. Even though Eastwood's option had been picked up by Universal after six months and his salary raised to $100 a week, it could hardly be said that, apart from the experience and the money, he was getting much out of his contract with the studio.

Never Say Goodbye (1956), a remake of *This Love of Ours* (1945) was a soggy tearjerker designed as a showcase for Universal's top star Rock Hudson, who played a doctor long separated from wife Cornell Borchers, before they finally came together again to make a home for their daughter, the while (no doubt) aisles filled with damp paper tissues. Yet again Eastwood, this time with four lines, played a laboratory assistant in one brief scene with Hudson. The critics ignored him and the film itself was described by the *Monthly Film Bulletin* as: '... competent in a woman's magazine way'.

After *Never Say Goodbye*, Universal said farewell to Eastwood when they failed to pick up his option after some 18 months. Ironically years later, as a superstar, he would base his Malpaso Company offices at Universal.

Eastwood now found himself as a freelance actor in a movie world more and more under the attack of television and facing rapidly shrinking audience attendance figures. His first movie after Universal looked, on paper, just the thing he needed to help his career take off, particularly since director Arthur Lubin, who had left Universal and gone to RKO, gave him a screen credit, 'introducing' Clint Eastwood for the comedy *The First Travelling Saleslady* (1956). By then, however, millionaire Howard Hughes was beginning to lose interest in RKO which he owned and, as it turned out, *The First Travelling Saleslady* was a real stinker. Ginger Rogers starred as Rose Gillray, who, after her corset-making company goes bankrupt, heads for Texas with her former model Molly, played by Carol Channing, to sell barbed wire for her largest creditor. Eastwood played a young rough-rider who attracts the interest of Channing but the movie's attempts at comedy misfired; and both audiences and critics failed to take much notice of the film, although the *Hollywood Reporter* commented: 'Clint Eastwood is very attractive. . .'

Star in the Dust (1956) at Universal was a routine Western directed by Charles Haas and toplined John Agar as a sheriff facing danger alone when he tried to hang a professional gunfighter. Again it did nothing for Eastwood's career, and the same was true of his second movie for RKO.

This was *Escapade in Japan* (1957) which once more reunited him with director Arthur Lubin, and which was finally released by Universal after Howard Hughes had closed down the RKO operation. Eastwood's role as a zany pilot Dumbo, whose part served only as a catalyst to the activities of two young children, was simply a bit one, the movie's nominal leads being Teresa Wright and Cameron Mitchell, and the plot itself barely demands more than a few seconds consideration being, as the *Monthly Film Bulletin* noted: '. . . really only an excuse to look at some lush Japanese backgrounds'.

The next two years were tough ones for Eastwood and during this period he even seriously considered abandoning a career as an actor. Indeed, it is likely that he made more money in 1957 and 1958 back at his old occupation of digging swimming pools than he did from appearing in front of the cameras. The studios were all rapidly retrenching under the increasing competition from the small screen and there was little in the way of meaty roles for unestablished freelance actors. So it was inevitable that, to survive, Eastwood would have to start working in television, even though in those days it was considered to be a big come-down for a movie star to turn to acting on the small screen. He played parts in 'Highway Patrol', 'Men of Annapolis', 'Navy Log' and 'West Point', in which he made several appearances and, if these performances did nothing to forward his career, they were at least preferable to labouring.

It was to be television, however, that was to bring stardom to Eastwood but, before that happened, he made two more feature films, one of which he himself described as: 'It was the lousiest Western ever made.' Harsh words indeed but, if not absolutely the worst, *Ambush at Cimarron Pass* (1957) stands high among the ranks of the worst horse operas ever filmed.

Made for Twentieth Century-Fox and filmed in some 12 days, *Ambush at Cimarron Pass*, directed by Jodie Copelan, cast Eastwood as a villain in a routine Western about a group of Union soldiers who are forced, under the command of Scott Brady's Sergeant Matt Blake to join forces with a band of ex-Confederate soldiers taking rifles through hostile Indian territory. What entertainment there was came from the frequent incursions by Apache Indians and the movie remains a highly forgettable piece of work, although for *Monthly Film Bulletin* it was: '. . . a generally entertaining Western, despite the fact that neither direction, photography nor acting display any distinctive virtues'.

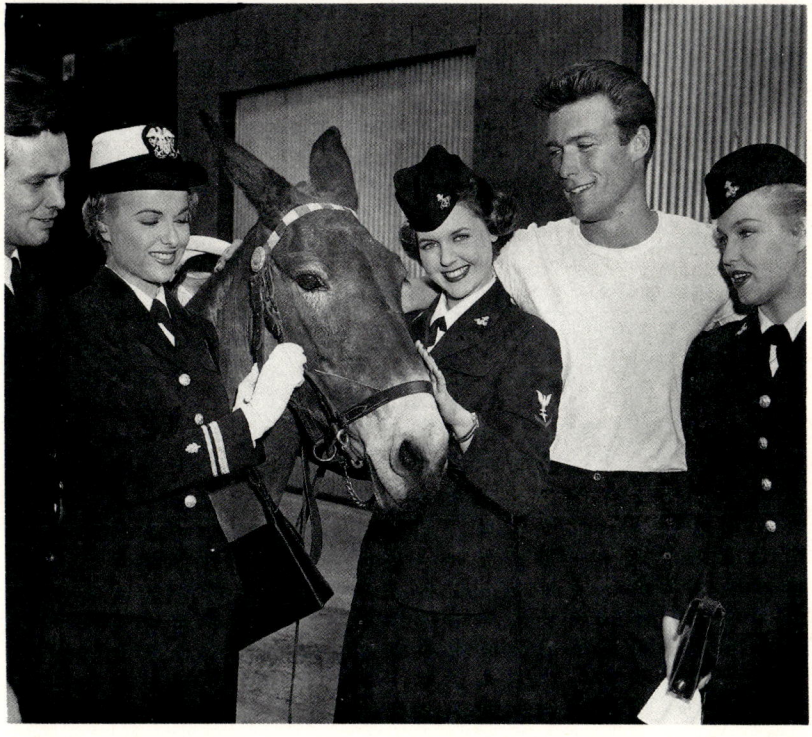

Francis the talking mule was the 'star' of a series of films in the 1950s, one of which, *Francis in the Navy* (Universal-International), afforded Eastwood a small part. With him and Francis are, from left, David Janssen (an early screen friend of Eastwood), Martha Hyer, Jane Howard and Leigh Snowden.

Eastwood and his wife Maggie arriving at the Los Angeles Music Center for a Motion Picture and Television Relief Fund gala in 1971 which raised $800,000 for the entertainment charity.

Lafayette Escadrille (GB: *Hell Bent for Glory*) (1957), Eastwood's final film during this depressing period, was a distinctly better film, made for Warner Brothers. It reunited Eastwood with his old friend David Janssen, whose option Universal had also failed to take up at the time that they had dropped Eastwood. And, although his part as George Moseley was hardly the kind that stardom is made from – the film being designed to provide a vehicle for young Warner Brothers actors like Tab Hunter and Will Hutchins – it did give Eastwood a chance to work with a major director for the first time.

He was William Wellman, once a pilot, Foreign Legionnaire and actor, and who had been responsible for such major Hollywood movies as *Public Enemy* (1931), *Nothing Sacred* (1937), *The Ox Bow Incident* (1942) as well as the classic aviation drama *Wings* (1927), which made *Lafayette Escadrille* – which followed the fortunes, romantic and in the air, of a group of First World War fliers – the kind of movie that he could get the most from. However, while the playing of the youthful actors gave the movie a certain amount of life and spontaneity, the film never achieved its hoped-for epic quality and the flying sequences made a considerably bigger impression than did the performers. For Eastwood, *Lafayette Escadrille* was experience – but little more. Despite some vigorous publicity by the studio, the movie fared indifferently with the critics and failed to make an impact with the public.

With his failure to make any kind of break-through with his post-Universal pictures, it must have seemed to Eastwood that his movie career was grinding to a halt.

Once again, however, luck was on his side, even if it was to mean that he would have to defect – for a while, at any rate – to television and thus join the ranks of actors who were not only helping the enemy but more often than not, discovering a graveyard on the small screen.

RAWHIDE AND SPAGHETTI WESTERNS

Much has been made of Eastwood's good fortune at being at the right place at the right time in order to land his role in the television series 'Rawhide', and publicity releases about him put out by CBS Films Information Services during the run of the show tended to play up the fortuitous circumstances surrounding his casting.

For once, publicity hyperbole more or less matched the facts. Following his stint in *Lafayette Escadrille*, Eastwood once more found himself out of work. By chance he happened to be passing CBS Television City in Hollywood one day and decided to pay a social call on CBS Television Story Consultant Sonia Chermus, who was a friend of his and Maggie's.

What followed was worthy of the best Hollywood legends. At this time Westerns formed a popular staple of American television programming and CBS was in the process of creating a series to oppose the current hit 'Gunsmoke'. While he was talking to Sonia Chermus, Eastwood was seen by CBS Executive Television Producer Robert Sparks, who happened to come into the office. He asked Eastwood if he was an actor. On being told by Eastwood that he was, Sparks took him to meet 'Rawhide' producer Charles Marquis Warren, a writer and director who had created 'Gunsmoke' and was to go on to create 'The Virginian' for television, as well as to make a moderate career as a feature film maker.

Sparks and Warren had been in the middle of casting discussions to find a second lead to Eric Fleming, who had been cast as trail boss Gil Favor. Having elicited from Eastwood his previous screen credits, Sparks and Warren asked him to read a scene for them. Impressed by the result, they asked him to make a film test. After a week or so, Eastwood heard the good news: he had been chosen to play the younger cowboy Rowdy Yates in 'Rawhide'.

The formula of 'Rawhide' was a tried and tested one, encapsulating in its half-hour episodes a series of dramas centred around the two characters played by Fleming and Eastwood, along with a number of other regulars including Paul Brinegar as Wishbone the cook, Sheb Wooley as scout Pete Nolan, plus Steve Raines, Rocky Shahan and James Murdock.

The first episodes were filmed in Arizona and Eastwood enjoyed working on location with the genuine cowboys hired to add authenticity, and he was able to use his time on the series not only to increase his expertise as a rider but to hone his skills as an actor. He also observed the fundamentals of direction, something that was to stand him in excellent stead in the future.

However, after the first season's episodes had been completed, CBS, concerned at the plethora of Western series currently being shown on television, had cold feet about 'Rawhide' and decided to leave the series unshown. Eastwood was dismayed.

But luck was still on his side and the first episode of 'Rawhide' was finally transmitted on 9 January 1959 and became an overnight hit, making stars of Eastwood and Fleming. It was to run to 144 episodes and lasted from 1959 to its final telecast on 4 January 1966. Had it been filmed in colour, there is little doubt that, with Eastwood's subsequent immense popularity, it would have continued to be shown in syndication for considerably longer.

The television series 'Rawhide' first brought Eastwood to a wide public, running for seven years. A scene from one of its 144 episodes, showing Eastwood with Nina Shipman and James Best.

The straightforward cowboy image Eastwood portrayed in 'Rawhide'. As the series developed he refined the silent, tough character that eventually brought him success in the cinema.

In his role as Fleming's second-in-command, Eastwood began to develop the laconic, tough-guy character that was to be refined in many of his subsequent movies. According to publicity releases, he also insisted on performing his own stunts in the series, being quoted as saying: 'After all, this is an action show, and it's a lot more gratifying when I can perform the action myself instead of having a double do it for me. A lot of actors are in pretty good shape, but they aren't conditioned to long periods of hard physical effort. They get pretty tired towards the end of an active day, and it shows up in their performances. By my keeping in condition, it's a lot easier on the director – and on me. On the whole', he added, 'I'm glad I took up swimming and basketball and lumberjacking, instead of chess or bird-watching.'

'Rawhide's' success ended Eastwood's anonymity. He had to become accustomed to the goldfish-bowl life of an easily recognized star and to learn to deal with the deluge of fan mail he began to receive as 'Rawhide' climbed in the ratings. Financially, 'Rawhide' was just what he and Maggie needed and they were able to move from Sherman Oaks to a bigger and better home.

As 'Rawhide' continued its success through successive seasons, Eastwood began to chafe at the restrictions imposed on him as the star of a long-running series. His original contract with CBS had given him the option of guest slots on other shows as well as the chance to make feature films during the periods that 'Rawhide' was not being filmed but in the event, these promises were not kept and, in the *Hollywood Reporter* on 13 July 1961, his patience came to an end and he let rip. He was quoted by writer Hank Grant as saying: 'I haven't been allowed to accept a single feature or TV guesting offer since I started the series. Maybe they figure me as the sheepish, nice guy I portray in the series, but even a worm has to turn sometime. Believe me, I'm not bluffing – I'm prepared to go on suspension, which means I can't work here, but I've open features in London and Rome that'll bring me more money in a year than the series has given me in three.'

He and CBS made peace and Eastwood appeared on television chat shows, making it clear that he was open to offers for feature films. But his rebellion against the constraints of the series took on a new form.

Eastwood decided that he would like to direct, spurred by an occasion when the 'Rawhide' team were shooting a stampede sequence on location involving 3,000 head of cattle. He suggested that the director should let him go in among the cattle with an Arriflex camera to shoot really dramatic stampede footage. He did not get to film what he wanted on that occasion and later, although he pressed the producers and received Fleming's blessing, his request to direct an episode was similarly thwarted and he had to console himself when CBS finally allowed him to direct some trailers for the show.

'Rawhide' achieved immense popularity abroad as well as in the United States. Westerns were then popular and Italian director Sergio Leone, who, after working as an assistant to Italian film makers and to such American directors as William Wyler, Fred Zinnemann and Raoul Walsh when they made movies in his home land, had made his own debut as a director with *Il Colosso di Rodi* (US, GB: *The Colossus of Rhodes*) (1961), decided to make a Western version of the Japanese samurai epic *Yojimbo* (1961) which had been directed by Akira Kurosawa. No doubt confirming his enthusiasm for the project was the success of John Sturges' *The Magnificent Seven* (1960), which had been a re-working as a Western of Kurosawa's 1954 movie *Shichinin No Samurai (The Seven Samurai).*

During the 1960s a large number of American actors had been making a good living performing in Italian movies, mainly in the then currently popular sword-and-sandal epics and various other action pictures. Leone wanted an American for the lead of his proposed Western *Per un Pugno di Dollari* but he was constrained by the very modest budget of $200,000 available to him through the consortium of film companies – Jolly Film in Rome, Constantin Film in Munich and Ocean Film in Madrid, who were funding the movie.

That left relatively little money for the star. After contacting various American actors then working in Rome and finding that they were not available, actor Richard Harrison provided Leone with a possible solution when he suggested Eastwood for the leading role. Leone had not heard of Eastwood and so made an approach to James Coburn, who had been one of the stars of *The Magnificent Seven*. But Coburn asked for $25,000 which was too much for Leone's budget.

Leone then contacted the William Morris Agency in Los Angeles who were Eastwood's agents and that telephone call was to mark the beginning of Eastwood's career as a movie star. He accepted the role of The Man with No Name and flew to Spain to make *Per un Pugno di Dollari*, arriving in Almeria in May 1964.

Filming was complicated by the fact that, although the script was in English, Eastwood

himself spoke no Italian and was the only English-speaking actor in a cast that included Gian Maria Volonte (billed under the pseudonym Johnny Welles), and Continental actors Marianne Koche, Pepe Calvo and Wolfgang Lukschy. But, despite all the problems of communication that accompanied the making of the film, it resulted in a Western of considerable bloody power and one that was to catalyze the genre and to give impetus to the immense international popularity of what was to become known as the 'Spaghetti Western', a genre that would rework traditional Western themes and mores into a violent, bloody and uniquely Continental kind of film, which even Hollywood would prove unable accurately to reproduce.

The script for *Per un Pugno di Dollari* by Leone and Duccio Tessari remained fairly faithful to *Yojimbo* with the setting changed to the small town of San Miguel, where laconic and mysterious stranger Eastwood arrived on a mule to precipitate himself into the bloody rivalry between the two opposing gangs – the Baxters and the Rojos – who held the town in their thrall.

Eastwood's character, with his unshaven face, unlighted cheroot clenched between his teeth and the grubby poncho that was to become a trademark of his stardom, was destined to achieve almost iconographical status. In next to no time, The Man with No Name, having accurately summed up the situation, remarks that 'There's money to be made in a place like this' and proceeds to do just that, working for both the Rojos and the Baxters and playing one faction off against the other so that, after the ensuing bloodbaths, he is left alone and alive and ready to ride off into the sunset in the true tradition of the Western.

What gave *Per un Pugno di Dollari* its real power and popularity with film-goers was that characterization was reduced to the simplest terms, dialogue was kept down to a minimum and the emphasis was placed on the kind of unremitting action, violence and gunplay that was almost a parody of the Hollywood Western. But, more than anything else, it was Eastwood himself, dominating the movie with his sheer presence and terse underplaying that hid the coiled spring of violence within the character, who ensured the incredible success of the movie.

When he completed the film, however, and returned to Hollywood, he had no idea that it was to mark a watershed in his career. He continued to make episodes of 'Rawhide' and occasionally to tell amusing stories of his Spanish summer on television talk shows.

He, and the producers of *Per un Pugno di Dollari* who had initially low expectations of the movie, were totally unprepared for its reception. The movie was duly released in Italy and received, at the start of its screen-

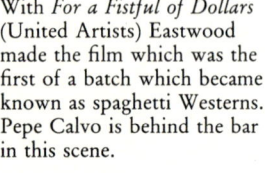

With *For a Fistful of Dollars* (United Artists) Eastwood made the film which was the first of a batch which became known as spaghetti Westerns. Pepe Calvo is behind the bar in this scene.

The hat, the poncho and above all the cheroot which earned him the sobriquet 'El Cigarillo' in Italy. The quintessential Eastwood character in *For a Few Dollars More* (United Artists).

ings, a low-key reception. But, after a few months, it was a runaway hit, taking more money in Italy than had *Mary Poppins* and *My Fair Lady*. Before long, it repeated that success in the rest of Europe.

Eastwood's catapulting to stardom – outside the United States, at least – was confirmed and, known as *El Cigarillo*, he became Italy's biggest box-office attraction. Even in South America his popularity was such that he was dubbed *El Pistolero con los Ojos Verdes* (The Gunman with the Green Eyes). Definitely a prophet without honour in his own country, where he was famous simply as the star of television's 'Rawhide', Eastwood had to wait for the movie's release in the United States.

The producers of *Per un Pugno di Dollari* had failed to obtain the United States rights to *Yojimbo* and it was not until 1967 that the movie, now known as *A Fistful of Dollars*, was released in America, by United Artists. And, as so often in the cinema, the critics failed to like the movie, although, as usual filmgoers knew better.

His second movie made with Leone, *Per Qualche Dollari in Piu* (1965), titled for its English language release *For a Few Dollars More* to cash in on the first film's title, was on its first release in the United States at the same time, so there was plenty for critics to get their teeth into.

Time was scathing, saying: '... *Fistful* should have been a loser from the word *avanti*. Instead it has become the fastest draw in Italy, outgrossing *My Fair Lady* and *Mary Poppins*. So far, it has made some $7,000,000 in Europe and spawned two equally hot sequels, *The Good, the Bad and the Ugly* and *For a Few Dollars More* – which earned Eastwood a few dollars more, jumping his salary from $15,000 per picture to $250,000. Whatever his financial arrangements, actor Eastwood, the sometime star of television's 'Rawhide', is certainly not paid by the word. In *Fistful* he hardly talks at all. Doesn't shave, either. Just drawls orders. Sometimes the bad guys drawl back. Just as tersely. Trouble is, after they stop talking, their lips keep moving. That's because the picture is dubbed. Like the villains, it was shot in Spain. Pity it wasn't buried there.'

Said the *Saturday Review*: 'While the picture lacks the subtler characterizations of its prototypes it does have fully as much gore ... Eastwood as the stranger, makes full use of his one expression, dangles a cheroot from the corner of his mouth, and, with two sequels already on the way, is obviously going to replace the ageing John Wayne. It is obvious, too, that the American Western is not dead; it has merely gone to Italy. Sergio Leone meet John Ford.' For the *New York Daily News* it was: 'a straining-hard-to-be-off-beat almost pop Western; not bad enough to be bad or good enough to be good'; and *The Observer* noted: 'The calculated sadism of the film would be offensive were it not for the neutralizing laughter aroused by the ludicrousness of the whole exercise.' But the *Daily Mail* commented percipiently that it was: '. . . a cruel but memorable picture'.

Eastwood himself was more sanguine, noting later, apropos the huge box-office records set by *A Fistful of Dollars:* 'Of course I was delighted. Some actors say they don't care about box office ratings, but not me. I care. I like to play to a full house and entertain a crowd', and he told *Variety* that he saw the character of The Man with No Name as: '. . . the kind of anti-hero who does what everybody would secretly like to do . . . a kind of Bogart in the saddle – who is not afraid to be himself, good or bad'.

In 1965 CBS dropped Eric Fleming from 'Rawhide' and Eastwood's character became the series' star as trail boss, while Fleming made *The Glass Bottom Boat* (1966) with Doris Day and accidentally drowned in the Amazon while filming the pilot for a television series 'High Jungle'. But Eastwood's days on television were rapidly drawing to a close and he starred in only 22 episodes as trail boss before the final episode was transmitted on 4 January 1966. That same year a feature entitled *The Magnificent Stranger* (which had been the shooting title for *A Fistful of Dollars*) was released: it turned out to be an edited version of two 'Rawhide' episodes and was promptly suppressed. There was a subsequent attempt to do the same thing with *El Gringhero*.

In 1965, Eastwood returned to Spain to make his second Western for Leone, reprising his character of The Man with No Name in *Per Qualche Dollari in Piu (For a Few Dollars More)*, this time receiving a fee of $50,000 plus a percentage of the profits. The budget of $600,000 was enough to pay for another American actor, Lee Van Cleef, as the bounty hunter Colonel Mortimer who joined forces with Eastwood to hunt down the crazy, drug addicted villain El Indio, played by Eastwood's co-star from *A Fistful of Dollars*, Gian Maria Volonte. The movie, scripted by Leone and Luciano Vincenzoni, was very much the bloody mixture as before, with even more violence than its predecessor, since *A Fistful of Dollars* had proved triumphantly at the box-office that the public was willing to take as much overt mayhem as they were offered.

For a Few Dollars More (1965) was released by United Artists in the United States at the same time as *A Fistful of Dollars*, and like that film, stormed the box-office.

For *Time*, the film was: 'For those who like an elemental western with galvanic gestures, a twanging score full of jew's-harps and choral chanting and a lofty disdain for sense and authenticity, the film will be ideal.' Writing about Eastwood and Van Cleef, the *Sunday Times* critics Dilys Powell said:

The Good, the Bad and the Ugly (United Artists) was the third spaghetti Western made by Eastwood and directed by Sergio Leone. Eastwood was 'the Good' and the success of the previous films allowed the budget to afford a third American actor, Eli Wallach, who played 'the Ugly'.

Lee Van Cleef, with his back to the camera, played 'the Bad' in *The Good, the Bad and the Ugly* (United Artists). In this scene Eastwood is being about as active as some critics suggested he could get when not actually killing, that is, he is lighting his cheroot.

'... the partnership produces, especially in the latter part of the film, moments of what an indulgent judge might possibly call vigorous crude action. Now and then there is something almost operatic in the complex of orchestral uproar and solo bang-bang', but went on to note: 'I still find the whole thing repulsive and degrading.' The *Evening Standard*, too, found a lot to dislike, commenting: 'The Italians certainly know how to shoot a vicious Western but soon one notices how the film veers to what you could call the pornography of violence. That's to say, death is only relished for the kick it gives.... Each falling body is rung up like a cash register, or a box-office ticket. On the audience, too, the film is likely to prove injurious. It has the shrillest, loudest soundtrack in recent memory, one that drills you neatly between the eyes. Reach for your aspirin bottle, pardner.'

Regardless of critical reaction, however, Eastwood was now firmly established as an international star, having survived a long-running television series which, all too often, proved to be the end of the careers of other actors who emerged from the small screen taste of stardom to find themselves typecast and basically unemployable. CBS settled his 'Rawhide' contract on 8 February 1966 and then he returned once more to Spain to make his third Spaghetti Western for Leone.

This was *Il Buono, il Brutto, il Cattivo* (1966) (*The Good, the Bad and the Ugly*) which again reunited him with Leone and Van Cleef and which cast Eli Wallach as the film's third American star. This time he was to receive a salary of $250,000 and a percentage of the profits, and, playing 'The Good' of the title, he even had a name this time – Joe. The screenplay was written by Age Scarpelli, Luciano Vincenzoni and Leone (there were to be no more mistakes like the copyright problem that had held up the American release of *A Fistful of Dollars*) and once again the movie repeated the successful mixture of action, violence and gore that had characterized its predecessors, this time on a much bigger budget of $1,200,000. Eastwood, Van Cleef ('The Bad') and Wallach ('The Ugly') found themselves immersed in violence and gunplay in their search for $200,000 of stolen gold.

Leone certainly intended the movie to be an epic Western to end all Westerns. In Italy it ran for some three hours and, cut by more than 30 minutes for its English language release it was still an overlong affair, redeemed by Ennio Morricone's attractive score when the going became tedious. The movie gave Eastwood a chance to perfect his stillness and apparent lack of dramatic pyrotechnics that was to lead to director Vittorio de Sica dubbing him as: 'absolutely the new Gary Cooper'.

Said the *Monthly Film Bulletin:* 'A sharp, cynical Continental Western which would have been a good deal more enjoyable if it hadn't been so determined to rise above its stylistic station.... All the characters are strictly two-dimensional, but Clint Eastwood and Lee Van Cleef are impressively

Eastwood in *The Witches* (United Artists), the last of his Italian films, in which he starred in an episode entitled *A Night Like Any Other* with Silvana Mangano.

impassive, while Eli Wallach has a high old time sneering and grimacing in a valiant attempt to make a lovable rogue out of the double-crossing Tuco.' *The New York Times* noted: 'I'm one of the few people I know who will publicly admit to having liked the Sergio Leone, Italian-Spanish Westerns that made Eastwood an international star. In those spare, bloody, nihilistic nightmares, photographed in the powdery colours of the Almeria desert, Eastwood's fathomless cool was framed with style. The movies required absolutely nothing of him except that he exist, the perfect physical spectre haunting a world in which evil was as commonplace as it was unrelenting.'

This is to downgrade Eastwood's acting abilities. He was not just simply there, but a cool, still eye in the centre of violent hurricanes, and he gave his three pasta pictures a solid centre which raised them above the level of mere exploitation pieces filled with guts, gore, gunplay and near-unmotivated violence.

Eastwood was to make one more Italian film, appearing in one of the five segments of the almost unreleased *Le Streghe (The Witches)* (1966) appearing in the episode *Una Sera Come Le Altre (A Night Like Any Other)*, under the direction of Vittorio de Sica, playing Silvana Mangano's dull husband. Then his pasta period was over.

THE ONE EXPRESSION OF STARDOM

Now that he was an established international star and had no financial worries, Eastwood and Maggie bought a home and land near Carmel on the Monterey Peninsula and settled down, finally starting a family when their son, Kyle Clinton, was born on 19 May 1968. Eastwood, not too seriously, was quoted as saying that by then he and Maggie knew that they could get on well enough and that they could now be sure of their relationship.

Eastwood had yet to make a major American picture and he found that in Hollywood he was still being regarded as a television actor. He also had to face the prejudice attached to American actors who, in Hollywood's view, were undermining their own film business by working abroad in foreign pictures.

United Artists, who had distributed the three Sergio Leone Westerns, realized that they were on to a highly successful box-office formula and so cast Eastwood in the lead of an American equivalent of the violent spaghetti Western, 1967's *Hang 'Em High*, for a fee of $400,000 and 25 per cent of the net profits. And those profits were considerable as *Hang 'Em High* scored at the box-office. Its success, with that of the recently released *A Fistful of Dollars*, *For a Few Dollars More* and *The Good, the Bad and the Ugly* put Eastwood into the top earners lists in both the United States and Britain.

Eastwood now carried enough muscle with movie producers to be able to ask that one of his one-time 'Rawhide' directors, Ted Post, should direct *Hang 'Em High*, marking Post's feature film directorial debut.

Hang 'Em High, written by producer Leonard Freeman and made on a budget of $1,600,000, attempted to rework the formula of the spaghetti Westerns within the context of the traditional Hollywood product. While the movie was as violent and brutal as the movies it was aping, and was a huge success with the public, it failed to achieve the feeling of the Leone films. Eastwood played Jed Cooper, a man unjustly convicted of murder and strung up to be left for dead by the lynch mob. But he survives the hangman's rope and sets out on a bloody odyssey of vengeance against his would-be killers as well as determining to prove his innocence. The script allowed Eastwood a more defined character and even a brief romance with Inger Stevens but what ensured its success was its action, violence and overt sadism. Filmed in Las Cruces, New Mexico, *Hang 'Em High* also featured Ed Begley, Pat Hingle and James MacArthur.

Eastwood's first film in America after the spaghetti Westerns was an attempt to continue the successful violent formula and *Hang 'Em High* (United Artists) was a success at the box office. Eastwood and Ed Begley in chains, threatened with the noose.

By now, as far as the public was concerned, Eastwood was critic-proof. In the *Daily Sketch*, Robert Ottoway was enthusiastic, writing: 'The cult of Clint Eastwood, star of those Italian Westerns that deal out violence like small change, has so far escaped me. He is so tongue-tied that every word seems likely to cause a rupture, and those half-opened eyes look as if he is about to collapse with inertia. But now he has taken his boots and saddle to America for *Hang 'Em High* and the change of scene suits him. He is still sullen and remote, but with a touch of Robert Mitchum in his swagger, of Gregory Peck in his frugal smile. Above all, he is one of the few cowboys now active who is not wheezing with middle age.' *The Observer* noted that: 'Clint Eastwood is a true descendant of the great Western heroes: lean, lank, tight-lipped, able to silence a saloon bar simply by walking into it', although the reviewer also commented that: 'There is mighty little pleasure to be gained from unmitigated brutality.' For *The Guardian*, *Hang 'Em High*: '. . . deserves at least one cheer for trying'.

It was at this time that Eastwood formed his own production company Malpaso (allegedly named from the Spanish for 'a bad step' which had been Eastwood's manager's comment when the star accepted his role in *A Fistful of Dollars*) and it must have afforded Eastwood a great deal of wry pleasure that initially its offices were located at Universal Studios, where not that long before he had been unceremoniously ejected when the studio failed to pick up his option. The company, first set up as a vehicle to provide Eastwood's services to other film-making companies and help alleviate his taxes, was run by Robert Daley with Irving Leonard – Eastwood's business manager – as president. Eastwood had met Daley in 1954 when the then accountant lived in the same apartment block and both were based at Universal Studios. Later, Daley was to produce all of Eastwood's movies and Sonia Chernus came over from CBS as script editor, Eastwood having never forgotten that she had been instrumental in getting him the role of Rowdy Yates in 'Rawhide'.

Hang 'Em High was followed by Eastwood's first major movie with a contemporary setting, the very enjoyable thriller *Coogan's Bluff* (1968). The movie cast Eastwood as a laconic and resourceful Arizona deputy sheriff sent to New York to bring back a criminal for trial. Finding that his way is constantly impeded by police and red tape, Eastwood tracks him down through the city in the traditional manner of a Western lawman, finally, after an exciting chase on a motorcycle, capturing him. In *Coogan's Bluff*, Eastwood was able to demonstrate his considerable abilities not only in action scenes but by more than holding his own against such seasoned performers as Lee J. Cobb, as the New York police lieutenant who proved such a thorn in Eastwood's side.

Coogan's Bluff benefited from a crisp script by Herman Miller, Dean Reisner and Howard Rodman and taut direction from Donald Siegel, who had come on to the film after the original director, Alex Segal, and Eastwood had parted company before filming began. It was Eastwood's first picture

Above: When he arrived at London's Heathrow Airport in 1967 Eastwood was met by a trio of glamour girls, Sandra Marshall, Sue Melody and Anita McGregor, who all seem impressed with the pistol-toting star. The ponchos look better on them, but not, perhaps, the cigars.

Right: Not the way Arizona deputy sheriffs are usually pictured, but Eastwood presumably has no complaints about his delicious armfuls of Melodie Johnson in *Coogan's Bluff* (Universal).

Eastwood showing his skill on the pool table. Boots and cues are the available weapons for one of the obligatory scenes of violence in Universal's *Coogan's Bluff*.

with Siegel, who had something of a cult reputation as the maker of such films as *Invasion of the Body Snatchers* and *Riot in Cell Block Eleven*, and who had been selected after being recommended by director Mark Rydell.

Coogan's Bluff was another success for Eastwood and also marked the break into the big time with a commercial hit for Siegel, with whom Eastwood was to establish an excellent working relationship on further films, including *Two Mules for Sister Sara* and *Dirty Harry*.

Critics, as well as the public, liked *Coogan's Bluff*, marking an auspicious beginning for Malpaso's involvement in Eastwood's films. Said the *Daily Sketch*: '. . . this is an original, exhilarating, superbly raw-boned variation on the old Western theme', going on to conclude: 'If you're disappointed in it, then I'll consider any reasoned request for a refund of your ticket money', while *The Sun* described the film as: '. . . a sharp little number which spits out wisecracks as frequently as broken teeth and balances its hot violence with a nice line in cool sex. Clint Eastwood . . . emerges here as an actor of considerable personality and humour, not to mention sex-appeal.' The *Daily Mirror* wrote of Eastwood: 'giving his best performance yet . . .', and in the *Daily Express*, Ian Christie commented: 'You could have no one better than Clint Eastwood, the bloodstained hero of those Italian Westerns, to play the part of

Above: *Where Eagles Dare* (MGM) cast Eastwood and Richard Burton as a United States/British team ordered to rescue from the Germans a general held captive in a castle in the Alps, and featured dramatic adventures on a cable car.

Right: A keen motorcycle enthusiast with bikes of his own, Eastwood took the opportunity during a break in filming *Where Eagles Dare* at Elstree Studios in England to test run a 150-mph 750-cc Norton at Brands Hatch – and ordered three, two for James Garner and one for himself.

the innocent abroad', adding: 'It's a pleasure to see an accomplished cowboy without his horse, for once, holding his own among the city slickers', and *Time* noted: 'Eastwood, who has hitherto displayed nothing more than a capacity for iron-jawed belligerency in a series of Italian-made Westerns, performs with a measure of real feeling in the first role that fits him as comfortably as his tooled leather boots.'

His next picture, a campy Second World War adventure tale that was as enjoyable as it was improbable, was *Where Eagles Dare*, written by best-selling author Alistair MacLean and filmed on location in Austria and England during 1968. The movie, made by MGM, gave top billing to Richard Burton, who badly needed a success after a period when his films had been doing poorly, and most of the attention he was receiving came from his marriage to Elizabeth Taylor. Eastwood received $800,000 for the picture and, despite initial misgivings, he and Burton got on splendidly together. Burton summed up his co-star's measure as an actor when he was quoted as saying: 'He has a kind of dynamic lethargy, he reduces everything to an absolute minimum.'

Where Eagles Dare was ripe melodrama, packed with action and directed, at a cracking pace that propelled the movie over the glaring implausibilities of its plot, by Brian G. Hutton. In it Eastwood played a tough professional assassin from the United States Army who joins forces with British major Burton in order to attack a supposedly impregnable castle high in the Bavarian Alps and rescue an American general held captive by the Germans. Characterization, logic and sheer common sense were subordinated to the action and driving narrative, and the resultant movie was in the best tradition of all those old Saturday morning serials. It succeeded in giving Burton's career the boost he wanted but, in the acting stakes Eastwood, both in his 'dynamic lethargy' and as a man of action, won the honours hands down.

Eastwood had enjoyed himself in Britain making *Where Eagles Dare* and that enjoyment transmitted itself into the completed film, which turned out to be yet another of his successes at the box-office, although not this time with the critics.

Said the *Daily Mirror*: '*Where Eagles Dare* is technically a well-manipulated piece of tosh which will make a mint at the box office. If it suffers from the current film malady of being too long, at least it keeps pitching at the audience's solar plexus. The laconic, deadpan Clint Eastwood, laden with fuses, bullets, and bombs conscientiously follows the director's instructions and his performance is a golfing eagle – two shots below

Left: Eastwood got on well with Burton during the making of *Where Eagles Dare*, but doesn't seem too comfortable with the Pekinese he met aboard Burton's and Liz Taylor's yacht *Beatrix*.

Eastwood mountain-climbing in *Where Eagles Dare* (MGM). Later he made *The Eiger Sanction* and developed a deep respect for mountaineers.

par.' For *The Guardian*'s Richard Roud it: '. . . would be terribly boring were it not so silly' and the *Evening News* commented: '. . . thrilling as the action is, Alistair MacLean's story is the most dreadful piffle.'

If *Where Eagles Dare* had been fun to make, *Paint Your Wagon*, which Eastwood made on loan from Malpaso for Paramount and director Joshua Logan, most certainly was not.

On paper, the omens for the movie must have looked good. Logan was the respected

Right and below: Two scenes from *Paint Your Wagon* (Paramount). Made in Panavision and Technicolor, with a wealth of talent both in front of and behind the camera, it promised a sure-fire success, but was disappointing. Tough guys Eastwood and co-star Lee Marvin both sang with some success, but the box office returns were disastrous.

director of such movies as *Picnic* and *Bus Stop* and the musicals *South Pacific* and *Camelot*. And not only was Eastwood now at a peak of popularity but he was to be partnered with another top star, Lee Marvin. The screenplay was written by respected writer Paddy Cheyevsky and based on the smash hit Broadway success of Frederick Loewe and Alan Jay Lerner, who had been responsible for *My Fair Lady*. And, since *The Sound of Music* had proved to be a phenomenal draw at the box office all over the world, it must have looked impossible to Paramount that *Paint Your Wagon* could fail.

But fail it did – and disastrously. First Paramount found that they could not have their original choice for leading lady, Julie Andrews, who decided to make the musical *Darling Lili* for her husband Blake Edwards, also for Paramount. Instead, the studio cast Jean Seberg, hardly a draw at the box-office in the role of Elizabeth, the woman who marries prospector Lee Marvin but finds out too late that she is expected to live in a *menage à trois* with his younger partner, the part assigned to Eastwood.

Unfortunately, little about the movie came together. The plot and motivations were unconvincing and the film, plagued by problems, went far over budget. Its failure, and that of *Darling Lili*, nearly caused Paramount to go into bankruptcy.

For Eastwood it must have been something of a nostalgic return to the location in Oregon where years earlier he had been a lumberjack. But it could not have been long before the tensions and traumas of filming *Paint Your Wagon* convinced him that he was about to make his first unsuccessful movie since *A Fistful of Dollars*. Writing in the *Los Angeles Times* on 22 July 1968 columnist Joyce Haber said: '... Logan is in so much trouble on Lerner's and Paramount's big budget musical that they're saying from Hollywood to Baker, Ore., that

Eastwood putting a pool table to conventional use (compare page 31). During a break in shooting *Paint Your Wagon* in Baker, Oregon, he took Jean Seberg to the Silver Dollar Saloon, where she looks doubtfully at his strange left-handed cueing action.

35

he's about to be replaced. Likeliest candidate for Logan's job, Richard Brooks who directed last year's *In Cold Blood*.' In the event, however, Logan completed the picture.

Despite the arthritic tedium of *Paint Your Wagon*, Eastwood emerged as one of the best things in the film, surprising those who did not know that he had already made records with a singing voice, modesty described by himself as: '. . . not exactly Howard Keel, but I think it'll work'. And it did, as his performance of the songs 'I Talk to the Trees' and 'I Still See Eliza' proved. Improbably, it was Lee Marvin's throaty rendition of 'I Was Born under a Wandering Star' that became a hit in Britain.

Inevitably, *Paint Your Wagon* (1969) died at the box office and critical comment was largely against it, although the *Los Angeles Times* wrote: 'Among the performances, Clint Eastwood's stoic and handsome dignity stands out, and he sings in an unscholarly baritone, which is fine.' And the *Monthly Film Bulletin*, which liked the score and Nelson Riddle's orchestrations commented: 'If *Paint Your Wagon* is less painful than it might have been – and it is – it is small thanks to Joshua Logan, who directs with his usual stagebound reliance on pretty compositions, so that the film tends to look like a series of picture-postcards dissolving into each other.'

While he had been making *Where Eagles Dare*, Eastwood had established a good friendly relationship with Elizabeth Taylor, who had accompanied Burton for the filming, and she had passed on to Eastwood a script she had been sent entitled *Two Mules for Sister Sara*. He liked it and the two agreed to make the film together and Universal then bought it.

But, when *Two Mules for Sister Sara* (1970) started shooting in Mexico, Elizabeth Taylor was no longer available and Shirley MacLaine (who received top billing on the picture) was cast as the prostitute, who is forced to masquerade as a nun in Emperor Maximilian's Mexico and is saved from rape by Eastwood as a Texan cowboy. Eastwood was quoted as saying that the picture: '. . . is really a two-character story and the woman has the best part – something I'm sure that Shirley noticed. It's kind of *African Queen* gone West.'

Two Mules For Sister Sara marked Eastwood's second film with director Donald Siegel and was the least effective of their pictures together, turning out to be a lacklustre affair in which the uncomfortable mixture of violence and comedy never succeeded in integrating. To add to Eastwood's disappointment at not making the film with Elizabeth Taylor, filming was plagued by illness which struck most of the cast and crew, including MacLaine who ended up in bed with a bad case of 'flu. Only the perennially healthy Eastwood remained unaffected.

Said the *Daily Sketch:* 'Clint Eastwood, acting as always as if he's groping for dark

Right: Eastwood searching for a likely place to put a short-fused stick of dynamite in *Two Mules for Sister Sara* (Universal), in which he helps guerilla forces fight the French in the Mexican revolution.

Far right: Clint Eastwood back in his best-known guise of the unkempt loner posing before some cacti in *Two Mules for Sister Sara* (Universal).

Shirley Maclaine as a prostitute masquerading as a nun (a role originally intended for Elizabeth Taylor) co-starred with Eastwood and some impressive Mexican scenery, including this fine array of bells, in Universal's disappointing *Two Mules for Sister Sara*.

glasses even when it's night, is traditionally heroic. In his way he can do with a twitching cheek muscle what Gielgud does with "Hamlet".' The *Daily Express* liked the picture, commenting: 'It is an entertaining work, and under the direction of Don Siegel it moves along at an unflagging pace', while *Time* noted that: '. . . the violence in *Two Mules For Sister Sara* is typically visceral. Siegel's talents, however, are weighed down by a heavy script and unwieldy performances by the two stars. Eastwood looks grizzled, stares into the sun and sneers, but anything more demanding seems beyond his grasp.'

Kelly's Heroes (1970) was the last movie that Eastwood would make that was not for his own Malpaso Company. He spent five months filming Troy Kennedy Martin's story which had enough echoes of the box-office blockbuster *The Dirty Dozen* to ensure that Eastwood was on to another commercially very successful picture. Eastwood took the leading role of one Private Kelly, who persuades an oddly assorted bunch of fellow American soldiers to join him in 'liberating' $16,000,000 of Nazi gold from a bank still held by the Germans – and all on a three-day pass. The movie – whose shooting title had been *The Warriors* – did not spend any more time than was absolutely necessary on exposition of the minimal plot and relied on casting – Eastwood, Telly Savalas, Don Rickles and Donald Sutherland – largely to take the place of careful characterization. The emphasis was on action and director Brian G. Hutton, who had made *Where Eagles Dare*, made sure here that the pace never slackened.

Eastwood was later to comment that *Kelly's Heroes* had not turned out the way he had hoped it would when he first read the script. Certainly the finished product was very much in the tradition of service life action dramas recently pioneered by *The Dirty*

Above: Eastwood starred with Don Rickles and Donald Sutherland in *Kelly's Heroes* (MGM), as Private Kelly, helping to relieve the Germans of millions of dollars, but was not satisfied with the finished film.

Left: Private Kelly, alias Clint Eastwood, at war in *Kelly's Heroes* (MGM), the last film he made in which his own company, Malpaso, was not involved.

Dozen and critical opinion saw nothing particularly special in it. Said *The Guardian*: 'After *Catch 22*, *Kelly's Heroes*. And if I may revamp the old phrase, better make it a long time after. Clint Eastwood's vehicle is about the same war, and makes a vague attempt to instil in the watcher the same sort of basic cynicism. All it succeeds in doing, however, is to leave a slightly disagreeable taste in the mouth, like chocolate-coated fishpaste. But perhaps one is being unfair. There wouldn't be much point in making a detailed comparison between *M.A.S.H* and *Where Eagles Dare. Kelly's Heroes* is just an entertainment movie. All I can say is that it entertained me for about half an hour of its 143 minutes and was much too noisy to doze through the rest of the time.' The *Daily Express* thought: 'The film is a conventional blood-and-bullets epic, but it is redeemed by the characters involved and by the way they are played. Clint Eastwood, as Kelly, continues to make a living by using the one expression at his command. . . .'

Eastwood the family man, with his first child, son Kyle Clinton, born in 1968. He was always anxious to keep his family life well away from the publicity spotlight.

DIRECTING, GOTHIC HUMOUR AND VIOLENCE

A key year for Eastwood was 1971. In many ways, it marked the most significant stage in his career since he had made the breakthrough to international stardom in the 1960s with his three spaghetti Westerns with Sergio Leone.

Following the problems that had attended the making of *Paint Your Wagon* and the film's subsequent failure, and the fact that, although a box-office success, *Kelly's Heroes* had not turned out to be the film that Eastwood had visualized when reading the script, he was now determined completely to control his own career through Malpaso, rather than to allow it to be subject to the judgement and execution of outside film makers.

It was, inevitably, a decision that had many detractors, who predicted that Eastwood would prove literally the meaning of Malpaso by taking what many considered to be a wrong step. Already many other stars had turned to producing their own vehicles and had come to grief and there were plenty of people in Hollywood who predicted that the same fate was in store for Eastwood, a view underlined by the fact that Eastwood was willing to turn down lucrative film offers in order to go ahead with his own projects.

That Eastwood's detractors would be proved spectacularly wrong is now a matter of historical record. He was able to show that he had a near uncanny ability to choose the right subject at the right time and, while some of his movies failed to receive critical approval, they did receive approval where, given the economics of film making, it really counted – with the paying customers. And 1971 saw him making his debut as a director, marking perhaps one of the most exciting phases in an already remarkable career.

Eastwood made three films for Malpaso in 1971. The first of these was *The Beguiled* which reunited him with director Don Siegel for the third time and which was triumphantly to demonstrate Eastwood's skill as an actor in a movie that is one of his best. It was also to prove to be a major work in Siegel's own canon.

Eastwood's role in *The Beguiled* was a distinctly atypical one, which, along with Universal's subsequent vacillation over the promotion and distribution of the picture, may well account for the fact that the film failed to attract the usual mass audiences for an Eastwood vehicle, instead achieving something of a cult status.

In his previous films, Eastwood had consistently portrayed characters who were completely in command both of themselves and the situations in which they found themselves, best exemplified by the three spaghetti Westerns he made for Sergio Leone and the larger-than-life heroes of *Where Eagles Dare* and *Kelly's Heroes*.

Eastwood, dressed for Californian weather, arrived in chilly London in January 1971, and immediately left for Rome. He had just been named most popular male film star in a survey by the Hollywood Press Association.

Right: *The Beguiled* (Universal), produced by his own company Malpaso, was a departure for Eastwood, in that he played the victim of the film, and required a wider range of acting ability than he had hitherto shown.

Below: Eastwood talking to director Don Siegel during the making of *The Beguiled*. It was their third film together, and Siegel remains the most influential of Eastwood's directors.

In *The Beguiled*, however, the character played by Eastwood was the complete opposite of everything he had previously essayed. This time he was victim rather than initiator and, if the switch of roles was to prove largely unacceptable to audiences, it did provide him with excellent opportunities – all very well taken – to extend his range as an actor and impressively to prove that he was not simply an action performer.

The screenplay for *The Beguiled*, written by John B. Sherry and Grimes Grice and based on a novel by Thomas Cullinan, gave Eastwood the role of John McBurney, a wounded deserter from the Unionist forces in the American Civil War found in the woods outside the Farnsworth Seminary for Young Ladies in Louisiana. The two spinsterly women who run the school – impeccably played by Geraldine Page and the younger Elizabeth Hartman – take him into the establishment in order to treat his badly wounded leg and nurse him back to health before turning him over to the Confederate forces. But his presence among the repressed inmates of the school acts as a potent sexual catalyst, not only among the impressionable pupils but, more dangerously, attracting the attentions of Hartman. Before long, he has created a dangerous atmosphere of sexual tension, hatred and jealousy which finally leads to his downfall, triggered off when Hartman catches him in bed with one of the students and takes physical action against him which results in the reopening of the wound in his leg. And, in what is clearly a metaphor for castration, Page amputates the unconscious McBurney's leg, and his ultimate death at her hands, further motivated by his drunken threat to disclose the existence of the school to Unionist troops camped nearby, becomes a tragic inevitability.

The Beguiled emerges as a powerful Gothic piece replete with elements of sexuality, repression and revenge, in which Eastwood is totally at the mercy of both his circumstances and the people he finds himself trapped with. It is perhaps one of the most subtle and stylish horror movies of the decade, with a pervasive atmosphere of claustrophobia enhanced not only by the performances of Eastwood, Page and Hartman but also by Siegel's meticulous direction and stunning cinematography by Bruce Surtees, particularly in the establishing location scenes outside the Farnsworth Seminary. Given considerably more dialogue than in

Eastwood did not direct *The Beguiled*, but maintained a deep interest in the techniques of directing, and in his next film directed himself.

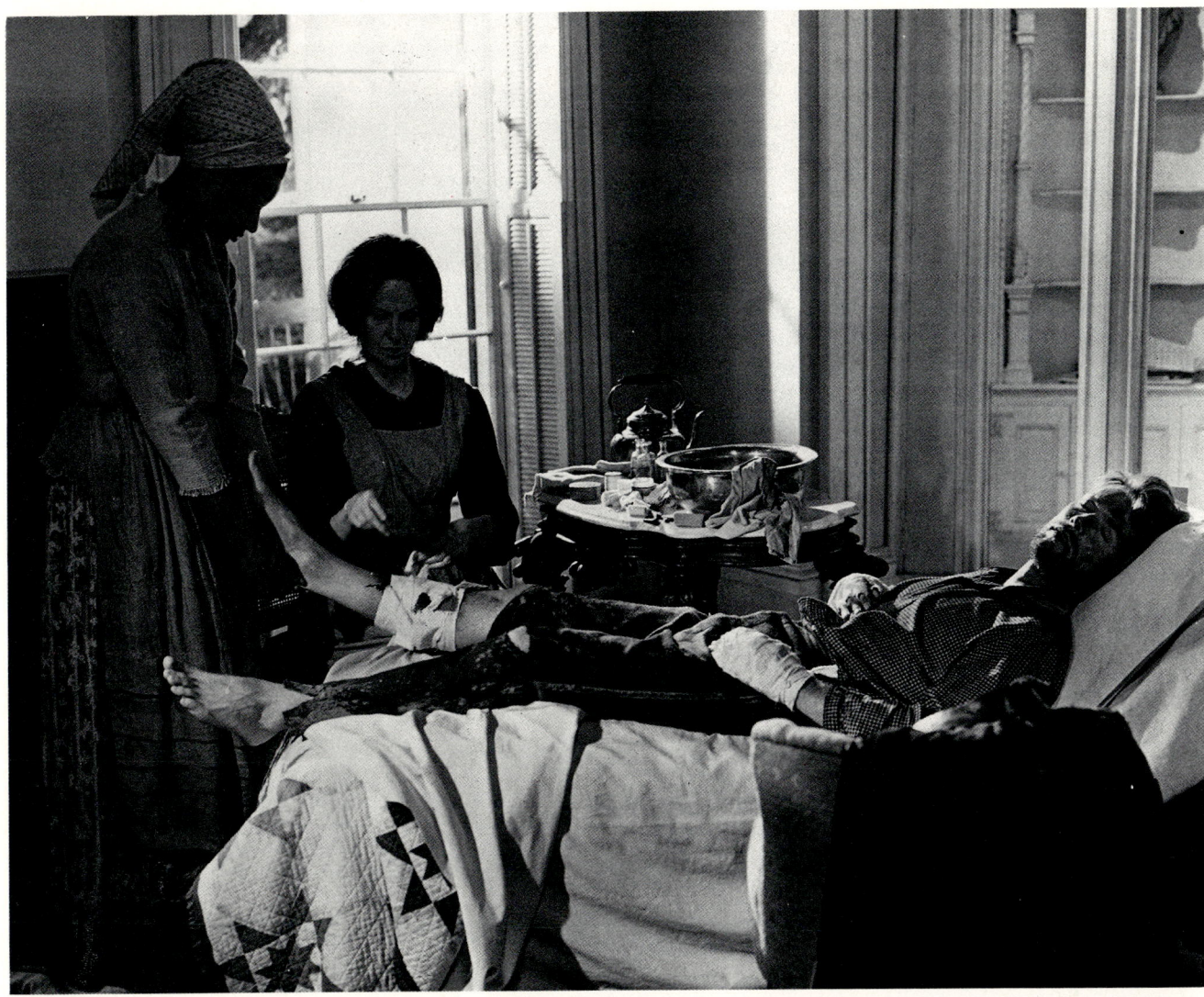

his previous movies, Eastwood acquits himself superbly and, in casting Page and Hartman, he succeeds in coming up with a movie in which there is not a single weak or under-developed element.

Critically, if not financially, *The Beguiled* was a triumph for Eastwood, its chances of major success being destroyed by Universal's failure properly to launch the picture. Audiences were unsure as to just what kind of movie it really was and were unprepared for the skilful Gothic melodrama it turned out to be.

Said *The Times*: 'Somewhere around the middle of Don Siegel's *The Beguiled*, things take a very peculiar turn. Up till then it has been mainly a mood piece about war and its innocent victims, but suddenly it blooms orchid-like into a rarified piece of Southern Gothic. I am not sure that the change entirely works, but it does make for a remarkably beguiling film.' *Time* called it: '... a Southern gothic horror story that is the most scarifying film since Rosemary birthed her satanic baby', going on to say that: 'Eastwood, working with Siegel for the third time, exudes a cool, threatening sexuality. ...' The *Financial Times* thought it: '... a tale bizarre enough for Bunuel. ... The whole thing is managed with great address, well-paced, with atmospheres and undertones vividly and economically suggested, and a balance held adroitly between horror and *grand guignol* scepticism.' *The Guardian* thought it was: '... very odd ... Excellent playing and a real sense of time and place kept one gawping right up to the hell-bent ending. It is only afterwards that one realizes that perhaps one shouldn't have been so readily taken in.' And the *Hollywood Reporter* said of Eastwood that: 'The performances are uniformly excellent, with Clint Eastwood being the most impressive, particularly in the second half of the film in which he is called upon to break with the more passive dimensions of the role and demonstrate a greater versatility and range than his best past work has indicated.'

The year 1971 saw Eastwood as the number two box-office star after Paul Newman

Above: Slave woman Mae Mercer (standing) and Geraldine Page, headmistress of the Farnsworth Seminary for Young Ladies, tend the wounds on Union soldier Eastwood, whom they concealed from Confederate guards in *The Beguiled* (Universal).

Far left: The conflict in *The Beguiled* (Universal) arose from the potent feelings aroused by the wounded Eastwood in the sexually impressionable inmates of the girls' school in which he was hiding, not least Elizabeth Hartman, who helped run the school.

and he now felt that it was time to extend his capabilities and become a director, something that he had wanted to do since his long stint on 'Rawhide'. And, never one to take the easy option, he chose to make his debut not with what would have been an obviously 'safe' subject – namely a Western – but to direct himself in a tough thriller, *Play Misty for Me* (1971). Universal, who were to release the film, felt that Eastwood was stepping out of his range and insisted that he act in the movie without a fee, taking a percentage instead. The movie's success made it a highly profitable enterprise for the director-star.

Eastwood was quoted as saying that he made his directorial debut with *Play Misty for Me* because: 'It was a small story and lent itself perfectly to being shot on natural sets. Working in authentic and realistic backgrounds in Europe during my years there as an actor had taught me the value of utilizing such locations.' And, indeed, one of the many felicitous pleasures of watching *Play Misty for Me* comes from the well-used and perfectly integrated backgrounds, mainly the Monterey, Big Sur and Carmel areas where Eastwood himself lived and which he knew perfectly.

Eastwood's role in *Play Misty for Me* was that of a radio disc-jockey whose life is filled with all the women he wants, including his girl friend, played rather insipidly by Donna Mills. And each night during his stint behind the microphone, a woman rings in to ask him to play the Erroll Garner classic *Misty* for her. Later, not knowing who she is, Eastwood picks up Evelyn Draper – a scaringly credible performance by Jessica Walter – and takes her home from the bar for what he believes will be simply another one-night stand. But when she reveals that she is the constant caller asking for *Misty* and that she wants him for herself, suddenly fandom becomes something a great deal more sinister and Evelyn is revealed as a dangerous psycopath. And the movie develops a considerable measure of suspense and terror as she sets out ultimately to destroy him.

Play Misty for Me was a double triumph for Eastwood, both as actor and director. In his capacity as director, he displayed an immense talent that resulted not only in a film that totally succeeded as a top-notch thriller but he also demonstrated an unerring ability to control not only his own performance but also to get from Walter one that dominated her scenes, in no small measure due to Eastwood's complete unselfishness towards her participation in the film.

Don Siegel was also on hand again for *Play Misty for Me*, but not behind the camera. Instead, he had a small role as the barman Murphy which he played well, despite his nervousness at appearing in front of the camera.

Play Misty for Me would be a significant movie, regardless of its director, often achieving the kind of tension and unease that was the characteristic of Hitchcock thrillers and the climax was genuine edge-of-the-seat stuff. All in all, it was an impeccable piece of film making, done with an assurance that brought it in under time and under its $950,000 budget.

Time commented: 'On an informal Richter scale of movie terror, *Play Misty for Me* registers a few gasps, some *frissons* and at least one spleen-shaking shudder. A good little scare show, in other words, despite various gaps in logic and probability . . . Eastwood displays a vigorous talent for sequences of violence and tension. He has obviously seen *Psycho* and *Repulsion* more than once, but those are excellent texts and he has learned his lessons passing well.' In *The Times*, John Russell Taylor wrote: 'If Don Siegel had been directing this one can imagine that the accent would have been fairly and squarely on the suspense element: what will happen to the hero? Will the woman scorned get to his girl-friend before he does? But that is clearly not Mr Eastwood's way as a director. Indeed, the film could be accused of playing down that side of the story too much, building its melo-

Eastwood at the premiere of *The Beguiled* with a slightly earlier tough guy of the screen, Robert Mitchum.

The happy family enjoying a day in the sand in 1972. Clint Eastwood, Maggie and son Kyle.

Far right: The horror climax to *Play Misty for Me* (Universal) comes when the scorned fan Jessica Walter appears at the house of Eastwood's girl friend with a view to bloody mischief, and is followed by Eastwood who arrives in the middle of the mayhem.

Right and below: Two scenes from *Play Misty for Me* (Universal), which Eastwood directed and in which he starred as a radio disc jockey. Each night a mysterious caller asks him to play the classic 'Misty', and when Eastwood meets Jessica Walter for what he expects to be another short affair, she reveals she is the caller, and sinister events develop.

dramatic climaxes too slowly and when it comes to the point not letting rip enough. On the other hand, there are corresponding merits. The whole slow build-up of the relationship with the "Misty" lady in the opening sequences is beautifully done, as she gradually goes a little too far, assumes a little too much from a casual one-night encounter, degenerates from an irritation to a nuisance, and from a nuisance to a menace. The whole atmospheric side of the film is also strikingly well done, with its use of the unfamiliar suburban Californian coast, so much so that one can even overlook a couple of lyrical excursions into Lelouch country.... Altogether, a very promising debut for Clint Eastwood as director.' And *The Village Voice* claimed that: '*Play Misty for Me* marks a surprisingly auspicious directorial debut for Clint Eastwood...'

Dirty Harry (1971) was Eastwood's third film that year and probably the most successful – in box-office terms – of all his American movies. Its popularity was well deserved, since it gave the star a role that once again put him in complete control of everything about him and effectively transposed the self-sufficient loner of his Westerns into a well-realized contemporary environment.

The character of the cool, resourceful and ruthless San Francisco policeman Harry Callahan had originally been destined for Frank Sinatra but Sinatra suffered an injury to his hand which necessitated surgery and prevented him from going through with the film. Once again, Don Siegel directed from the powerful script by Harry Julian Fink, Rita M. Fink and Dean Reisner and the whole film was made on location in San Francisco with Eastwood performing many of the highly dangerous stunts himself.

Eastwood dominated *Dirty Harry*, giving a powerhouse performance as the tough Callahan in single-minded pursuit of a maniacal sniper whose motiveless killings hold San Francisco in a grip of terror. And, having apprehended the sniper (a chillingly unpleasant performance by Andy Robinson) he comes up against the law's red tape (much as he had in the excellent *Coogan's Bluff* a few years previously) which states that, having disregarded the killer's constitutional rights, his capture is invalid. The killer, set free again, returns to his reign of terror and this time, disregarding the niceties of police and legal procedure, Eastwood goes after him again and this time kills him. In a final sour coda, thoroughly sick with a legal system that appears to be loaded against lawmen and on the side of the criminal, Eastwood pulls off his badge and contemptuously throws it into the sea.

While *Dirty Harry* cleaned up at the box-office, there was the by now familiar undertow of critical discontent at the movie's violence and the implicit lawlessness of its vigilante theme. Apparently what was perfectly acceptable within the near-mythical confines of the Western was less comfortable when presented in modern dress and in an all-too-real contemporary setting.

Eastwood himself told *Variety*: 'I don't think violence sells. It has to be in the right story or the right situation. You can't just do action scenes and tack them together. What you do is tell the high points – I play a guy always on the edge of violence.'

The *Daily Express* commented: 'Directed by Don Siegel, the story is quite incredible and reasonably exciting. With policemen like Clint Eastwood and cowboys like John Wayne, civilization has nothing to fear.' The *Sunday Times* said: '. . . ingenious twists of plot, a splendid chase or two, and with a minimum of dialogue the director Don Siegel's mastery of narrative makes you share (deplorably, perhaps) the detective's rage at a law which ties the hands of the police and releases a murderer to murder again. Certainly it is violent. But if you want a thriller here it is – and quite as good as *The French Connection*.' And in the *Sunday Express*, the reviewer wrote that Eastwood gave his coolest, most effective performance to date, going on to say: 'Mr Siegel's film is undoubtedly violent, but it does not leave the nasty taste in the mouth that some more recent films have done. This is because the violence depicted is an integral part of a story which makes a serious comment on law enforcement in America today.' But *Variety* came down hard on the picture, saying: 'You could drive a truck through the plotholes in *Dirty Harry*, which wouldn't be so serious were the film not a specious, phoney glorification of police and criminal brutality. Clint Eastwood in the title role is a superhero whose antics become almost satire. Strip away the philosophical garbage and all that's left is a well-made but shallow running and jumping meller.'

This criticism was almost entirely to miss the point, both of the film and of Eastwood the star. Eastwood was providing for his audiences a superhero, someone intended to release them from their everyday worries.

Far left: Eastwood as Callahan in *Dirty Harry* (Warner Bros.), in which he tracks down a mad murderer who terrorizes the streets of San Francisco. It was a typical loner role as a vigilante for Eastwood.

Left: *Dirty Harry* (Warner Bros.) confirmed Eastwood's talent for knowing what the public wanted of him. It was action like this and violent scenes which troubled the critics but drew huge audiences to the cinemas.

THE RETURN OF THE LONE STRANGER

There are those stars whose popularity rests as much upon their often lurid off-screen lives as on their movie performances. Eastwood however, is the complete antithesis, always zealously guarding his private life from the sanctuary of his Carmel home. He spent as much time as possible between films with Maggie and his son. On 23 May 1972, his daughter Allison was born.

Even before the release of *Dirty Harry*, Eastwood was spotlighted on the cover of *Life* magazine, captioned: 'The world's favourite movie star is . . . no kidding . . . Clint Eastwood.' The accolade came about as the result of a poll carried out by the Hollywood Foreign Press Association. And, while he was still second to Paul Newman as a box-office favourite in America, the release of *Dirty Harry* at the end of 1971 would take him triumphantly to first place.

After the triumph of *Dirty Harry*, Eastwood returned to the Western with *Joe Kidd* (1972), made on location in California and Arizona under the direction of veteran John Sturges who had been responsible for such movies as *Bad Day at Black Rock*, *Gunfight at the O.K. Corral*, *The Magnificent Seven* (like Eastwood's *A Fistful of Dollars*, a reworking of a Japanese samurai movie as a Western) and *The Hour of the Gun*.

Eastwood took the title role of a tough cowboy – very much in his well established loner mould – who was hired by land baron Robert Duvall to hunt down a gang of renegade Mexicans, only to find himself caught up in a moral dilemma in which neither his employer nor his quarry appeared to have total right on their side. Unfortunately, the script by Elmore Leonard was over-complex and Sturges' direction lacked drive. Apart from an exciting sequence in which Eastwood drove a locomotive off the rails to career through a saloon, the movie emerged as yet another variation on his by now standard lone stranger character, and only the ever-reliable Bruce Surtees' magnificent cinematography retained any lasting impact.

Monthly Film Bulletin's comments were largely typical of the critical consensus on *Joe Kidd*, saying that it had: '. . . its moral landscapes so thoroughly confused that its attempts to strike some serious attitudes within a professionally executed entertainment leads only to a kind of no-man's-land of wasted professionalism. The Eastwood role, for instance, is superficially in the line of the actor's post-*Dollar* films, where the super-efficient individual with no goal, not even the lure of bounty, becomes the first victim of his own readily exploitable talents.' *The Village Voice*, however, although not liking the film itself, noted that: 'Eastwood manages to hold our attention with the same brand of humorously low-keyed, bottled-up violence that Sturges evoked with Steve McQueen in *The Great Escape* almost a decade ago.'

Oscar-winning writer (for *The French Connection*) Ernest Tidyman provided the script for Eastwood's next picture *High Plains Drifter* (1972) and, with Eastwood directing himself, it turned out to be among the very best of his 1970s films. Certainly its basic premise, cleverly held back until the movie's climax, gave *High Plains Drifter* an additional charge which not only set it apart from the general run of Eastwood's own Westerns, but marked it as a unique genre movie whose supernatural quality pervaded the atmosphere from the start.

As with his spaghetti Westerns, the character played by Eastwood in *High Plains Drifter* was another man with no name, simply known as 'The Stranger' who rides into the American Southwest frontier town of Lago and, when he is picked on by three men in the saloon, casually guns them down. Not surprisingly, given this vivid proof of his prowess with a gun, the Stranger is asked by the townspeople to help defend the town against three men set on avenging themselves against the people of Lago who framed them and sent them to jail. Agreeing, the Stranger appoints a dwarf as his deputy, orders all the houses in the town to be painted red and the name of the place to be changed from Lago to Hell. The climactic shootout results in the death of the three men and the near destruction of the town by fire – and, at the film's climax, it becomes clear that the Stranger is

Left: Clint Eastwood and Stella Garcia find time for a laugh in the course of hunting down renegade Mexicans in *Joe Kidd* (Universal/Malpaso).

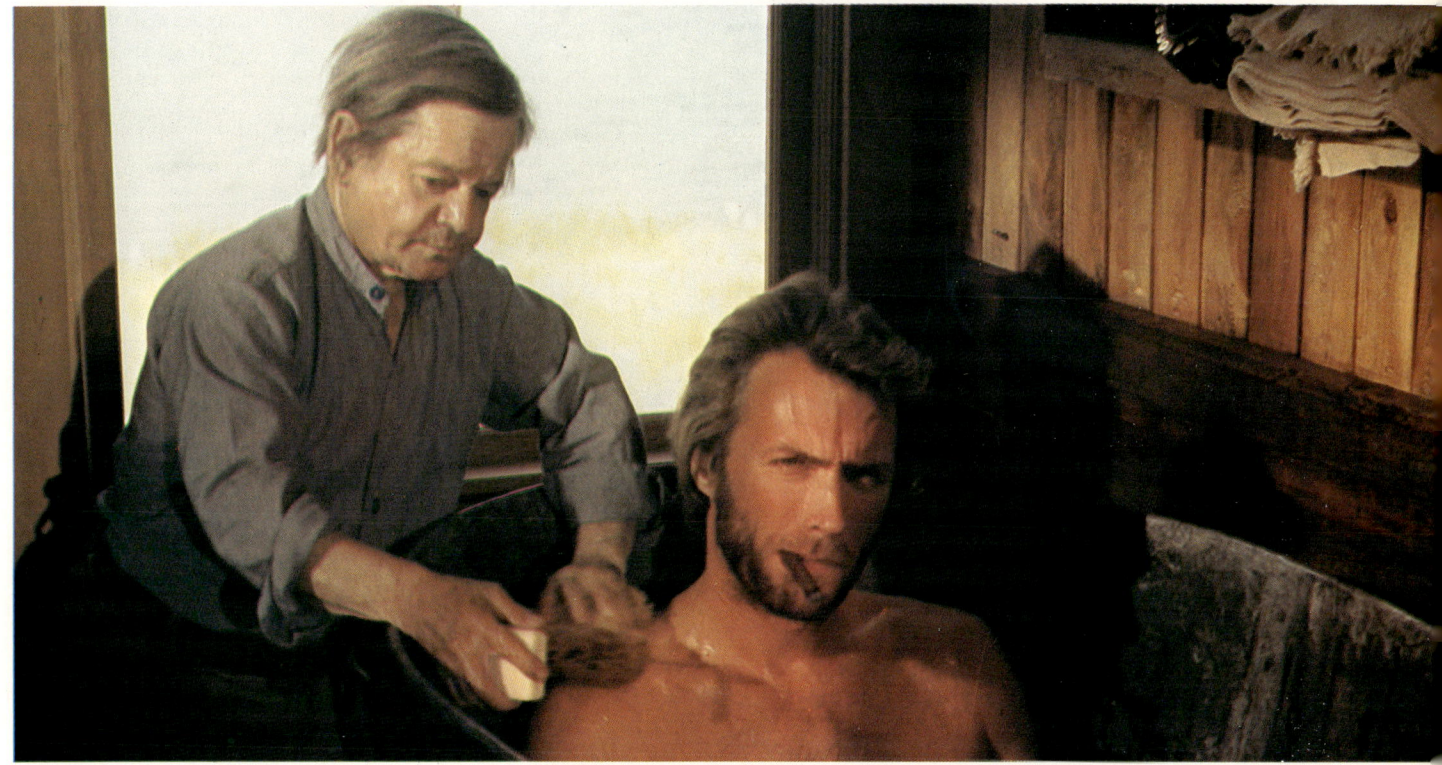

no ordinary man but in fact the town's former marshal Jim Duncan, who has returned from the grave after being whipped to death, finally to claim his vengeance.

Given this basically bizarre premise, it says much of Eastwood as both star and director that *High Plains Drifter*, stylish, occasionally tongue-in-cheek and suffused with the kind of violence – justified by the story – that was by now one of the actor's trade marks – should turn out to be such a good and satisfying movie. Shot on location at Mono Lake and, as was usual with Eastwood, brought in on time, on budget and without the tensions and histrionics so often associated with the isolation of location shooting, *High Plains Drifter* is an off-beat, exciting and often exhilarating piece of work.

While the public, as usual, enjoyed the movie, critical approval was generally lacking. In the *Daily Express*, Ian Christie wrote: 'Eastwood himself directs this uneasy mixture of bloodstained realism and peculiar fantasy adequately enough, but the result is

Billy Curtis, playing a little man despised by the folk of the frontier town of Lago, naturally helps the stranger, Clint Eastwood, when he visits the barber shop in *High Plains Drifter* (Universal).

simply rather silly. I suppose you could call it a supernatural Western, except that there is nothing natural about it and it certainly isn't super.' *The Times* commented: 'Eastwood rather overdoes his personal mystique, too; but enough of his old master Don Siegel's influence has rubbed off to make him an effective and promising commercial director.' *The Observer* thought it: 'Not at all a likeable film, but an impressive one', and *The Guardian* commented: 'Still, if you strip the movie of its turgid, heavily right-wing romanticism it remains an achievement. Eastwood, as *Play Misty for Me* indicated, is no mean director and he has the benefit of a tight, cynical screenplay from Ernest Tidyman, of *The French Connection* and *Shaft*, and some beautifully expressive camerawork from Bruce Surtees. The scene is stunningly set, the characters well-observed in one-dimensional terms. And Eastwood plays the avenger as if born to it, a Dirty Harry unshackled by silly liberal laws. It all works well, which is why one resents it so much. I can see the cineastes hovering over it like vultures over the body of the West.' And *Time*'s Richard Schickel drew his critical six-guns to let off with: 'This desperate inventiveness does not make a familiar tale interesting. It simply weighs it down under a load of cacophonously clanking symbols. As a director, Eastwood is not as good as he seems to think he is. As an actor, he is probably better than he allows himself to be. Meanwhile, the best you can say for *High Plains Drifter* is that the title is a low pun. Rarely are humble Westerns permitted to drift around on such a highfalutin plane. That, however, is small comfort as this cold, gory and overthought movie unfolds.'

Ted Post, who had directed Eastwood's first major American film *Hang 'Em High*, took the directorial assignment of making Eastwood's second movie about San Francisco cop 'Dirty Harry' Callahan when he put the star through the violent paces of *Magnum Force* (1973), from a script by John Milius and Michael Cimino, both of whom were to go on to careers as directors. Set once again in San Francisco, *Magnum Force* had Eastwood investigating a series of mysterious murders in the police department and once again there was a heavy emphasis on gunplay and violence. The movie was certainly efficient enough under Post's direction, and Eastwood gave his usual tough and accomplished performance, providing a solid centre to the movie which, as with all sequels, lacked the excitement – and in this case, the style – of the original.

The *Monthly Film Bulletin*, predictably for such an *auteur*-obsessed magazine and no doubt missing the presence of cult director Don Siegel or some other equally mythical figure upon which to base its assessment of *Magnum Force*, took a dim view of the movie: 'Milius, presumably, is responsible for the emphases which bring Western mythology, inherent in all the recent rough-justice thrillers, closest to the surface in *Magnum Force*: America is again felt to be so wide open that the individual with overwhelming charisma and uncommon dexterity with a firearm has more chance of tidying it up than the established forces of law and order. The result is much the same mixture as *Judge Roy Bean*, with Harry declaring laconically "Nothing wrong with shooting so long as the right people get shot", and the balance of power later tipping towards his opponents. . . . Not as mindless as *Walking*

High Plains Drifter (Universal) was a curious supernatural Western, directed by Eastwood himself, containing the usual violence and some tongue-in-cheek acting, but the risks were justified and the movie was a success.

Eastwood in *Magnum Force* (Columbia/Warner Bros.) again played 'Dirty Harry' Callahan tracking down a murderer amidst much gunplay and violence. It was a Western theme transferred to a modern police setting.

Tall, perhaps, *Magnum Force* turns out to be as much of an exploitative muddle.' And Eastwood came in for a pasting for his performance from the *Daily Express* which said: 'I know that policemen are supposed to remain calm in moments of stress, but Inspector Harry Callahan has more than just a stiff upper lip with which to confront a crisis. He has a stiff head and a voice as expressive as a vacuum cleaner's hum. But then, of course, he is played by Clint Eastwood who hasn't much of a reputation for the niceties of expression.'

Eastwood directed, but did not appear in *Breezy* (1973), a lightweight romantic drama which starred William Holden as a burned-out middle-aged man who regains his zest for life after an affair with a young woman, played by Kay Lenz. Jo Heims' script was hardly distinguished and, while Eastwood made the film with his usual professionalism and polish and elicited good performances from Holden and newcomer Lenz, *Breezy* had nothing about it to set it apart from any number of other movies with similar themes. What little interest it possesses derives from the fact that it is directed by Eastwood, although those who wholeheartedly espouse the *auteur* theory of film making might have a very difficult time guessing the name of *Breezy*'s director were it not on the credits of the film.

Said the *Financial Times*: '. . . there is nothing offbeat about *Breezy*, and nothing macabre except for the disturbing evidence it provides that no Hollywood director, however "virile" his talent in action films, seems capable of skirting sentimentality

Right: Eastwood directed, but did not appear in *Breezy* (Universal). Here he is explaining an unusual camera shot to the stars of the film, William Holden and Kay Lenz.

Far right: Eastwood catches the sun and forty winks during a break in the directing of *Breezy*, an undistinguished romantic comedy which itself represented a break from his usual themes.

Thunderbolt and Lightfoot (United Artists) was one of those partnership caper-movies made popular by *Butch Cassidy and the Sundance Kid*. The buddies were Eastwood and Jeff Bridges, enjoying himself in drag.

when dealing with stories of Love-across-the-Generation-Gap. (They should take a lesson from Fassbinder's *Fear Eats the Soul*).' The *Evening Standard* thought: 'A Love Story in which the over-50's can share? I suppose so, but for those of us in-betweens who won't see our teens again, it's got a lot of quiet amusement.' *Time* was happier with the movie, saying: '*Breezy* should be an ill wind but is not – not all the time, anyway. It is affecting in its weird little way. Maybe because it is pleasant to find anything animated by the romantic spirit at the movies these days. Maybe because William Holden has a saving, cynical sense of humour. Maybe because Eastwood has an easy way with actors that is far easier, more relaxed than his fussy way with the camera. But probably most of all because Bill Holden, 55, is still an astringent, no-nonsense sort of actor and his old-pro integrity is matched by the artless, awkward sincerity of newcomer Lenz.'

Michael Cimino, the co-writer of *Magnum Force*, made his debut as a director on Eastwood's next picture, *Thunderbolt and*

Lightfoot (1974), later going on to make the much lauded *The Deer Hunter* and the even much more villified megaflop *Heaven's Gate*. Cimino's script was very much in the mould of the 'Buddy' pictures exemplified by the Paul Newman–Robert Redford teamings in *Butch Cassidy and the Sundance Kid* and *The Sting* and cast Eastwood as Thunderbolt, a man on the run from his two pursuing ex-partners-in-crime George Kennedy and Geoffrey Lewis and rescued in the nick of time by Jeff Bridges' Lightfoot. The film soon developed into a crisp and enjoyable caper movie with Eastwood and Bridges finally joining up with Kennedy and Lewis to pull off the perfect robbery.

Cimino scored as both director and writer and *Thunderbolt and Lightfoot*, underpinned by Eastwood's powerful performance and a strong and likeable one from Jeff Bridges, is a slick, if overlong, thriller with a downbeat ending. On analysis, there is little to distinguish the plot from any number of other similarly written caper movies – except for the most important ingredient, Eastwood. His sheer presence, apart from the excellence of his performance, turns *Thunderbolt and Lightfoot*'s near-routine story into a thoroughly enjoyable piece of film making. Very few neophyte directors could have hoped to be as lucky as Cimino in his first film.

The Eiger Sanction (1975) was a disappointingly thin and routine spy thriller, with nothing much to differentiate it from the dozens of similar pictures that had been produced to try to cash in on the success of the James Bond movies. Apart from some pleasantly witty dialogue and a few enjoyable wisecracks, the screenplay by Warren B. Murphy, Hal Dresner and Rod Whitaker, based on a novel by Trevanian, held few surprises and not very much in the way of suspense until the climatic sequence set around a perilous climbing expedition tackling the north face of the Eiger.

Presumably it was this opportunity to work once again on absolutely realistic locations, something that had largely characterized his movies, that attracted Eastwood to the project. Certainly his role – that of a college art teacher recalled to the secret service and blackmailed into undertaking the assassination of enemies of the United States secret intelligence agency C2 – was painfully underwritten. Fortunately, once again his sheer presence imbued the part with characteristics not present in the screenplay.

Eastwood dishing out the religion in *Thunderbolt and Lightfoot* (United Artists). Eastwood and his colleagues in crime conspire to pull off the perfect robbery.

Above: *The Eiger Sanction* (Universal) was a routine spy thriller which gave Eastwood the chance to work on location in the mountains of Switzerland as he played an art teacher seeking out enemies of the secret service.

Far right: During the making of *The Eiger Sanction* (Universal), a stunt man was killed and Eastwood himself fell and disappeared from sight, suspended on the safety rope.

The challenge offered by the film – which Eastwood also directed – was the opportunity to shoot its action sequences on real mountains and not the usual studio papier mâché rocks backed up with process cinematography. So, before shooting began, he trained with experienced climber Mike Hoover for three gruelling weeks in California's Yosemite National Park but, even with this experience behind him, actual shooting of the mountaineering sequences on location in Switzerland proved to be hazardous in the extreme. British climber and stuntman David Knowles was killed by falling boulders on the Eiger and Hoover himself was hit – but not seriously hurt – during the same incident. Eastwood, as usual, took his own share of risks performing stunts for *The Eiger Sanction*. 'For one scene', he told an interviewer, 'I had to cut myself loose at 2,000 feet and drop down part of the way. It went fine but I fell on the safety rope which took me out of camera sight several hundred yards away. Everyone was worried when I disappeared.' He found in the professional climbers working on the picture elements very much in accord with his own character, being quoted as saying of the mountaineers: 'They are a breed apart. The thing about climbers that strikes you is the great camaraderie between them. You form friendships very quickly. You have to, because your life is in your partner's hands all the time.'

Critically, *The Eiger Sanction* came in for a panning from most quarters. However, with the power of its star, it soon went into profit, once again proving that the public went to the movies to see stars and were

largely uninterested in what critics had to say. *The Guardian* critic acknowledged this fact of cinemagoing, writing: 'It would be pretty surprising if *The Eiger Sanction*, based on Trevanian's popular novel, doesn't make a heap of money. It's one of those big formula movies that usually do very nicely, thank you. . . . But don't ask me to say it's a good movie. Clint Eastwood's pedestrian direction is only matched by a performance in the leading role that's about as frozen as the Eiger itself. Which is a pity, since Eastwood is undoubtedly capable of being a major presence on the screen – a latterday Mitchum who hasn't yet learnt that the best way to be appreciated is to depreciate yourself. But here he makes a boorish, self-regarding leading character forever posing in front of the camera as if about to seduce it with a handsome wink. And he doesn't even have to wink to get the girls in the picture', adding, however, that: 'The climbing scenes at least are good and the denouement spectacular enough to satisfy most lovers of this kind of adventure caper.' Said the *Daily Express*: 'Clint Eastwood directed this spy-thriller and the result shows he is much better coping with big chunks of rock than with actors. Mind you, the characters in this story are so shallow that nobody could have made them register on screen as recognizable human beings.'

Eastwood, a superstar who shuns the limelight, pictured in his California home with his son Kyle and daughter Allison.

STAR, ACTOR AND DIRECTOR

Eastwood was back in top form with *The Outlaw Josey Wales* (1976), the movie succeeding despite Warner Brothers' reservations that, at that time, Westerns were hardly doing well at the box-office.

Eastwood had not intended to direct as well as to star in the picture, the directorial assignment being given to co-writer Phil Kaufman who had come up with the screenplay with Sonia Chermus. However, Kaufman exited from the picture early on during location shooting and Eastwood, taking over, did a first-rate job.

The Outlaw Josey Wales had, for its romantic interest, actress Sondra Locke, who was to become an important part not only of Eastwood's repertory of Malpaso players, but of his personal life. She had made her screen debut in 1968's *The Heart is a Lonely Hunter*, earning herself an Oscar nomination for her performance, but her subsequent career, including roles in *Cover Me Babe* in 1969, *Run, Shadow, Run* in 1971 and *Willard* in 1972, had not lived up to that early promise. Here, under Eastwood's expert direction, she played a woman rescued from Indians by hero Wales and the two fall in love. Ironically, she had been considered, and rejected, for the Kay Lenz role in *Breezy*.

The Outlaw Josey Wales gave Eastwood an archetypal role, that of a peaceful farmer in post-Civil War America who, after the murder of his family by Union troops, becomes a vigilante, ending up with a price on his head as he journeys to Texas. The film was violent, although, as usual, the violence was integral to the story and not simply grafted on gratuitously, and Eastwood spoke to *Variety* on the subject, being quoted as saying: 'In the old type of Westerns, the heroes didn't want to get involved. But now I get involved right away. The audience thinks, "Wow, this is somebody to deal with", and they're waiting for more of it through the rest of the picture. I do all the stuff Wayne would never do. I play bigger-than-life characters, but I'll shoot a guy in the back. I go by the expediency of the moment', and he went on to distinguish the violence of his movies as being vicarious and cathartic and did not subscribe to the popular view that his movies appealed to audiences' baser instincts, because their violence arose from character and plot and was not simply included for its obvious exploitative value.

In *The Guardian*, Derek Malcolm wrote: 'The film is a curiously discursive effort, last-

'An army of one' sums up the Eastwood character in many of his films. In *The Outlaw Josey Wales* (Warner Bros.) he was a vigilante with a price on his head as he sought revenge on the Union troops who killed his family.

Above: Eastwood and Chief Dan George in *The Outlaw Josey Wales* (Warner Bros.). Eastwood won plaudits for his direction of the picture, but critics were beginning to point out an extreme right-wing philosophy in his film-making.

Right: The potential for violence is clear on the face of Eastwood, alias *The Outlaw Josey Wales* (Warner Bros.), as he follows the Western creed of a man's need to do what a man's got to do when his family is slaughtered.

ing two hours and fifteen minutes and reaching out increasingly into the area of myth as the story sputters to its admittedly healing close. It has been photographed with infinite care by Bruce Surtees in those same hills that so graced Arthur Penn's *The Missouri Breaks*. But Mr Eastwood is no Penn. As a moralist he is a great deal more clear-cut, not to say simplistic. A man, it seems to him, has got to do what he's got to do. Which tends to leave us watching the same thing *ad nauseam*. Even so, he is not a bad director, though his narrative drive is hardly as formidable as that of his real mentor Don Siegel. He has an eye for detail and a feel for authenticity that reminds one a little of Penn and encourages one to keep looking at the screen with the eye if not the mind. The mind, however, does come into it. Scratch an Eastwood movie and you'll find a political philosophy three paces to the right of Thomas Jefferson.' Like Wayne, Eastwood's movies were beginning to be reviewed as much for their political stance as for their entertainment value, something that, while providing a useful critical approach for those who enjoy that sort of thing, was something that was hardly likely to impinge on the consciousness – or enjoyment – of the major audiences for the star's movies.

The *Daily Express*, while saying that: 'You always know where you are with Clint Eastwood. He might not have much range when it comes to acting ability but when he is galloping over one with a six-gun in hand he makes a convincing Western hero', goes on to note that: '. . . it is an enormously enjoyable combination of excitement, tension and humour. Eastwood directed it himself and although it is over two hours long the rambling story holds your attention throughout. I could have ridden along with him all day.'

Eastwood returned to the character of Harry Callahan for the third time in 1976's *The Enforcer* but, although the movie proved to be immensely popular with movie goers, it was very much formula film making, despite the inclusion of a female partner – played by Tyne Daly – for Eastwood. He was back in San Francisco and violently in pursuit of a group of underground terrorists in the familiar milieu. For *The Enforcer*, Eastwood promoted James Fargo, who had been his assistant director on *The Outlaw Josey Wales*, to full director and Fargo, well understanding the formula elements that had made the previous two Harry Callahan movies a success, ensured that he did not stray from this winning streak, although the movie

The Enforcer (Warner Bros.) was the third in the Harry Callahan series, with Eastwood chasing terrorists in his usual violent manner. Audiences remained loyal to Dirty Harry and the film was another commercial success.

was nowhere in the same league as its predecessors.

'By now', said *The Guardian*, 'Harry Callahan looks an almost endearing figure, his right-wing chauvinism seeming scarcely more than a thinly-veiled joke... The whole thing is tight, light entertainment, splashed with blood and cynicism in the modern manner... If you like this sort of thing, it's a thoroughly professional example, with the Eastwood charisma carrying it all very easily on his broad, worn shoulders.' *Time* thought that it was: '... fairish fun – and certainly no threat to liberal democracy', while the *Daily Mail* also noted the mellowing of the character: 'I never thought I'd say it but welcome back "Dirty Harry"... What sensitivity he has, I suspect, is largely due to Clint Eastwood's consistently spare and magnetic performance... The film is slick, skilful, fast, unpretentious and it knows when to pull its punches... The final moments of the film are both poignant and bitterly funny. As I said, Harry is the man you love to hate – but you have to admire him, too.' And the *Sunday Times* noted: '... Dirty Harry is as exciting to watch as he would be appalling to encounter.'

Eastwood was back as director for his next picture, *The Gauntlet*, and Sondra Locke was back working with him again, this time as his co-star. The screenplay – by Michael Butler and Dennis Shryack – gave Eastwood the role of a laconic detective assigned to bring back a key witness in a corruption trial from Las Vegas to Phoenix – and, naturally, he has to survive and outwit attempts by Mob assassins to prevent the couple from making it back alive.

The movie provided a spectacular display of pyrotechnic mayhem which included the destruction of a Las Vegas bungalow into which policemen fired some 8,000 rounds of ammunition to reduce the place to rubble, the six-room wood and stucco building taking two weeks to construct and special effects men implanting some 8,000 explosive charges into holes drilled into the walls, fired on the director's command. And some £550,000 of the movie's over £3,000,000 budget were earmarked for the special effects – among which were a spectacular helicopter crash and the riddling by gunfire of Eastwood's 13-ton steel reinforced bus.

The Gauntlet may have been a modern fairy tale with Eastwood once again portraying the kind of tough and resourceful character that he had by now honed to perfection, and the romance between him and Locke's prostitute – who is also a college graduate – may have had more of wish fulfilment than reality about it, but it was also cracking good action entertainment and director Eastwood elicited a star-quality performance from Locke, while at the same time, presaging his later films with talented orang-utan Clyde, gently sending up his own tough guy image.

'Clint Eastwood doesn't say much', wrote William Hall in the *Evening News*. 'His face doesn't change expression very often. But he sure does a lot of damage', while *The Guardian* commented: '... it still manages to be one of the best American thrillers of an admittedly poor year. Eastwood as a director is now a real professional, and as an actor, only a fool would call him a slouch. Actually, he's a reactor, one of the best in the business just now. Sparing perhaps, but a look goes a long way. *The Gauntlet* is generally sparing too. It's a plain, honest-to-badness action thriller that's designed to

The Gauntlet (Warner Bros.) provided spectacle, with a large proportion of its budget spent on effects and with Eastwood playing another variation on his silent detective foiling the Mob.

appeal to a mass audience without insulting its credulity about the way things operate on the dark side of America. Admittedly the climactic sequence isn't actually very easy to believe in – the two drive a stolen bus through line upon line of firing police in order to reach the courtroom, with Shockley (Eastwood's character) finally walking past the credits despite at least two bullet holes. But you want to know what happens right up to the end. I reckon, at any rate, that Chandler or Spillane would have nodded an approving head.'

Creatively and financially, Eastwood was in the enviable position not only to be able to choose his vehicles but also to be able to turn down pictures whose themes or shooting schedules did not fit in with his plans. He allegedly rejected the opportunity to appear in the role eventually essayed by Paul Newman in *The Towering Inferno* and the lead in *Apocalypse Now*.

The old show business aphorism about never acting with animals or children usually holds painfully true. It says much for Eastwood's star quality that, despite a scene-stealing orang-utan co-starring with him, Sondra Locke and Ruth Gordon in *Every Which Way but Loose* (1977) it was he who dominated the movie, a delightful and funny film which proved that Eastwood was as adept at comedy as he had already shown himself to be at more macho screen pursuits.

Every Which Way but Loose, designed to change Eastwood's image without depriving him of any of the qualities which had made him the world's top movie star, was made at Warner Brothers studio in Burbank – where

Eastwood directed *The Gauntlet* (Warner Bros.) and co-starred himself with Sondra Locke, with whom he had a screen romance and who was to figure prominently in his private life.

Despite his tendency to repeat successful roles, Eastwood has shown a willingness occasionally to do something completely different, and his comedy *Every Which Way but Loose* (Warner Bros.), in which he 'co-starred' with an orang-utan, is an example. With the stars is director James Fargo.

Eastwood had moved his Malpaso offices from their first home at Universal – and was released by Warners as one of their two Christmas blockbusters for 1978, at the same time as their other big picture, *Superman*. And *Every Which Way but Loose*, the movie many thought would prove to be a disaster for Eastwood, ended up as the second most successful movie of 1979, understandably being beaten by *Superman*. Eastwood, now 48, was as big a box office draw as ever.

The script for *Every Which Way but Loose* was written by Jeremy Joe Kronsberg and directed by James Fargo, who succeeded in impressively combining the action and the comedy elements, as well as providing a music track attractively larded with Country and Western music. Since the movie required its star to box, Al Silvani, who had trained Sylvester Stallone for *Rocky*, was brought into the picture, finding the star to be a natural pugilist, able to perform impressively in the movie's fight sequences and, perhaps even more impressively, well able to hold his own against the naturally scene-stealing attempts by 11-year-old orang-utan Clyde.

In the film, Eastwood played California trucker Philo Beddoe, who supplements his income with some carefully engineered bare-knuckle fights promoted by Geoffrey Lewis' Orville, but spends most of the movie in amorous pursuit of Country and Western singer Sondra Locke, while himself being pursued by an over-the-hill gang of motorcycle Hells Angels led by the endearingly inept John Quade. Ruth Gordon contributed an enjoyably dotty performance as the crotchety Ma and the fun was fast and furious, well deserving its huge success at the box office.

Critics, however, failed largely to recognize the film's potential appeal to audiences. In the *Sun*, the reviewer commented: 'What on earth is Hollywood hard man Clint Eastwood doing monkeying around with an ape? Trying to change his image, that's what – with a comedy called *Every Which Way but Loose* in which he co-stars with a large orang-utan called Clyde. I give Clint six out of ten for trying, but he should have heeded the warning about never working with children or animals. He comes off best in most of the innumerable fist-fights, but a poor second in the comedy contest with Clyde. As for the ape, he should go far. I just advise him to pick his scripts a little more carefully in the future. . . The whole film is set in the brawling, beery world of the macho American male, crude in tone as well as language, and not really my cup of coke at all.' Said *The Observer*: 'In this picture, then, Eastwood appears to have set out to make some cock-eyed, snook-cocking statement in the form of a romp with his friends, in the way that John Ford and Howard Hawks improvised movies with their stock companies.

He's also tried to go even further down market in tone than his rival Burt Reynolds, and has produced a picture that's about as lyrical as a hard hat scraping on a corrugated-iron roof. . . But somehow a sporadically amusing film just doesn't jell, and as the private eye said in *Psycho*, if it doesn't jell you don't get aspic. What you get instead is something sticky and amorphous that doesn't stand up. Part of the fault lies with the script which is short on wit and logic, and long on scatology and random insult. Even more fault lies with the limp direction of Jim Fargo. . .'

Critics (and, as one myself, I have often found it out to my cost) rarely turn out to be right, except on purely artistic grounds. I saw *Every Which Way but Loose* for the third time in a small cinema in Marbella in Spain, in the company of my then host, movie actor Stewart Granger, and an audience largely composed of British expatriates with a sprinkling of Spaniards. *Every Which Way but Loose* proved to be highly popular with the great majority of those seeing it then, despite poor projection and muffled sound, and while Granger found it too long, most of the others I spoke to afterwards had seen the movie for what it was – professional entertainment of the most enjoyable kind, with a neat star performance from Eastwood.

Every Which Way but Loose effectively demonstrated what had already been evident in many of Eastwood's previous pictures – namely, that he possessed a deft and sure comic touch and that he was sufficiently secure in his screen persona to be able easily – and enjoyably – to send it up. Perhaps, more than anything else, the success of the movie demonstrated once more that Eastwood appeared to have an almost unerring touch when it came to choosing subjects the public would like.

Escape From Alcatraz (1978) was a direct descendant of all those tough prison dramas of the 1930s and 1940s that had, particularly, been one of the staples of the Warner Broth-

In *Every Which Way but Loose* (Warner Bros.) Eastwood played a trucker who earns money by bare-knuckle boxing, a comparatively mild form of violence for him.

Trouble in the famous prison for Eastwood in *Escape from Alcatraz* (Paramount), directed by his old friend Don Siegel and shot in Alcatraz itself, which needed a considerable face-lift for the occasion.

ers output whose roster of tough guy stars – James Cagney, Edward G. Robinson, Humphrey Bogart and George Raft among them – all served their screen time behind bars, more often than not being rewarded for their good behaviour with more of the same in subsequent movies. Now Eastwood was impressively to revive this particular film genre with a powerful performance that once more drew a satisfied response from the cinema-going public.

The screenplay for *Escape from Alcatraz*, by Richard Tuggle from the book by J. Campbell Bruce, was based on the true-life escape from the grim island prison by bank robbers Frank Morris, John Anglin and Clarence Anglin, who succeeded in getting away from Alcatraz on 11 June 1962. They were never subsequently found and it may well have been that none of the three escapees made it to freedom in San Francisco, although the movie had a suitably optimistic ending.

Eastwood told an interviewer: 'The moment I read it, I liked it. I tend to respond to a story on an animal level, and this appealed to me immensely. Frank Morris, the guy I play, was the leader of the breakout. All he ever dreamed about was escaping. There was another reason they didn't like having him there. He had a very high IQ. They knew that somebody that bright posed a threat.'

Escape from Alcatraz reunited Eastwood with director Don Siegel for their fifth film together and the movie gained considerable impact from the actual location filming in Alcatraz itself, which had long been closed down as a penitentiary but which was now a popular tourist attraction for visitors to San Francisco.

Having made the decision to film in Alcatraz, the film makers were faced with having to restore the place – now covered with the inevitable graffiti, the legacy not only of the constant passage of sightseers touring the place but also of an occupation of the island by a group of Indians some years previously who had been protesting against discrimination. Special paint, which could later be washed off without harming the original surfaces, was employed to bring the walls back to their original state and the unit were faced with replastering the crumbling walls themselves, repainting and installing new wiring and using heaters in an attempt to ameliorate the dank cold that pervaded the place.

Additionally, the shooting schedule had to be structured in order to take into account the constant flow of tourists, especially as

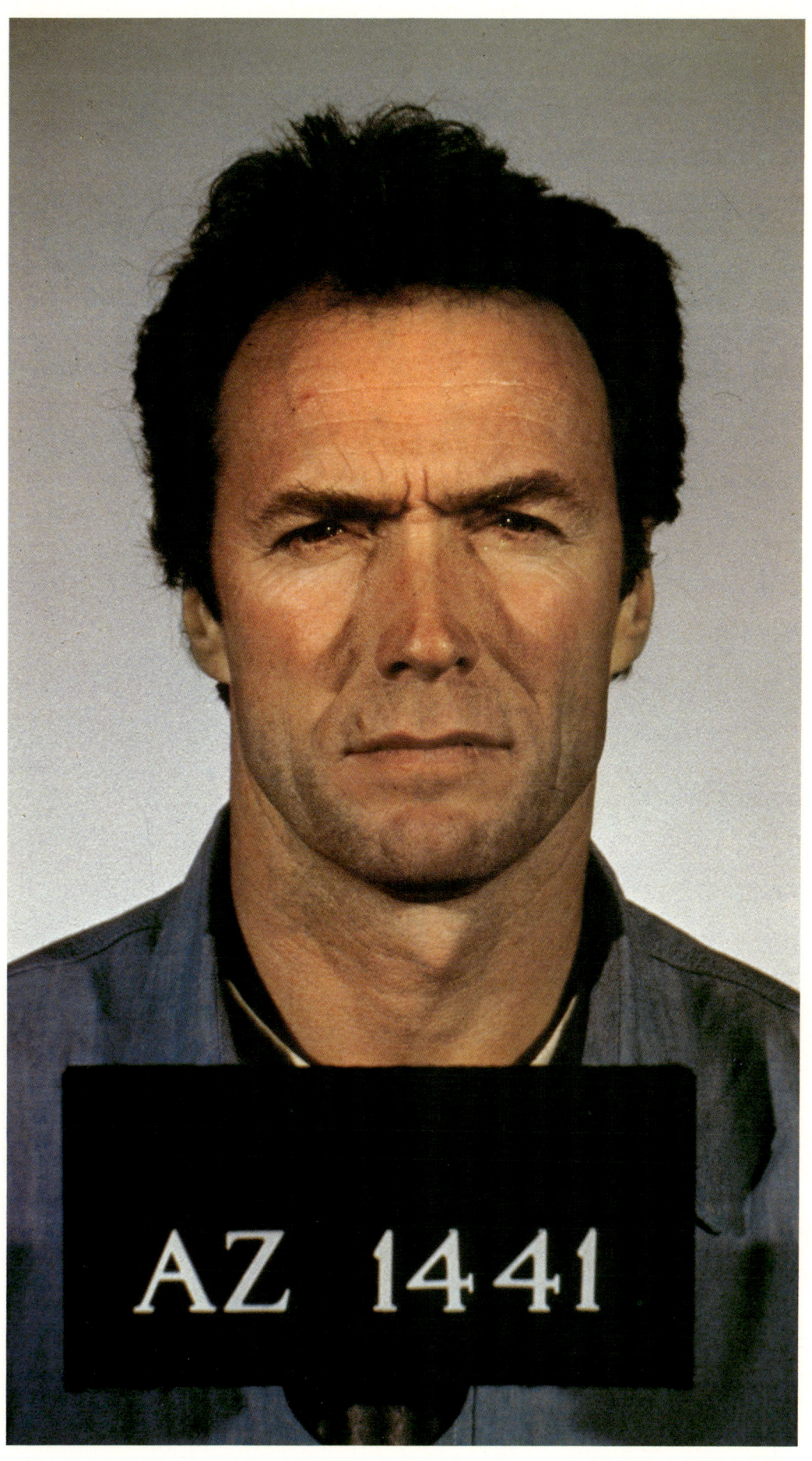

Prison portrait of Eastwood in *Escape from Alcatraz* (Paramount), a story based on a real-life escape of 1962 which had an unresolved ending which was tidied up for the movie.

Clint Eastwood with William Holden, whom he had directed in *Breezy*, after Eastwood had received a Life Achievement Award from the National Association of Theater Owners in February 1982.

the chance to catch a glimpse of America's top star was considerably more exciting than even the visit to Alcatraz itself.

The filming of *Escape from Alcatraz* must have been one of the toughest assignments undertaken by its star, given the appalling conditions of the location and the demands of the role. But Eastwood's insistence, as always, on as much realism as possible for his movies paid off once more and, while the movie was undoubtedly a grim and often chillingly bleak affair, it also contained one of his best and most sustained performances.

Said the *Evening Standard*: 'It is a familiar enough theme but, in Donald Siegel's deft and experienced directorial hands, the old yarn emerges with considerable vigour and a gradually building tension which sets the butterflies fluttering in the pit of your stomach when you least expect it. Eastwood plays a real character, Frank Morris, who actually did try to break out of the notorious escape-proof Alcatraz 20 years ago. But there is no attempt whatever to create a fully rounded, sharply observed character. Eastwood's talent doesn't run to detailed psychological perceptions and Morris might just as well be The Man with No Name, a brooding self-reliant enigma with few distinguishing personal characteristics except a distaste for authority, a twitching fist and a nice style in dry one-liners. It is the presence that counts, not the person.' Tom Hutchinson, writing in *Now* magazine said: 'From Eastwood, with minimal dialogue, comes a performance of great impact, an ability to suggest a man who has to break out before his mind breaks down. It is, perhaps, Siegel's most thoughtful contemplation of violence and the need that is argued for restricting it. It is also one of Eastwood's best roles for a long time. It is good to know that the old firm is back in business.' Said the *Sunday Telegraph:* 'Mr Eastwood's taciturn persona has rarely been

Eastwood is a good skier and in 1978 appeared in John Denver's celebrity ski race in Aspen, Colorado. Real life did not imitate the art of his films, and he lost.

better used . . .', and in the *New York Times* there was the adulatory comment: 'Mr Eastwood fulfils the demands of the role and of the film as probably no other actor could. Is it acting? I don't know, but he's the towering figure in its landscape.'

It was, of course, acting on the highest level and, even more so, a superb demonstration of star quality that many actors aspired to but few were able to achieve. Too many people take acting to be the kind of obvious display of technique which can easily be seen to be 'acting' in an almost theatrical sense of the word. Eastwood's abilities are far more impressive: not for him the blazing pyrotechnics of the 'traditional' actor, but a dominating, carefully thought-out performance whose very underplaying and precise qualities all too often tend to obscure the immense talent behind the kind of star acting that also relies impressively on reacting.

Eastwood had never been part of the 'Hollywood Scene' and zealously ensured that there were no unwanted intrusions into his personal life with Maggie and their two children at their Carmel home. He believed rightly, that what he owed his public were his on-screen performances and that his personal life remained his own affair. However, in 1979, the media had one of their Show Business holidays reporting that he and Maggie had separated over Eastwood's continuing relationship with his co-star from *The Gauntlet* and *Every Which Way but Loose*, Sondra Locke. And, in 1980, Eastwood and Maggie were divorced. Typically, neither took the opportunity to enter the kind of media arenas that usually accompany a major Show Business divorce, maintaining instead a dignified silence. Reportedly, Maggie received a $20,000,000 settlement, the $2,000,000 Carmel home and custody of 11-year-old Kyle and 8-year-old Allison.

Eastwood was back filming again in 1980, again co-starring with Locke in the excellent and strangely underrated *Bronco Billy*, which he also directed. The picture cast him as an ageing rodeo rider – who turned out not to be quite what he seemed – touring with his

Left: A second film with Clyde the orang-utan was *Any Which Way You Can* (Warner Bros.), in which Eastwood once again enjoyed himself, allowing the stuffy remarks of some critics to be drowned in the chink of the box-office returns.

Far left: Eastwood was honoured by the Deauville Film Festival of 1980, where *Bronco Billy* was entered in the official competition. With him in the rust-red outfit is his co-star and friend Sondra Locke.

Bronco Billy (Warner Bros.) was a comparative failure for Eastwood, audiences perhaps having seen enough of him guying himself in comedies, although the film, in which he was a rodeo rider, was actually quite good.

small-time circus tent show giving Wild West shows in small towns around the American mid-west and south and barely contriving to keep the venture one jump ahead of his creditors. Into this arrived Locke, playing a spoiled rich-bitch heiress presumed to have been murdered but actually on the run from her stuffy husband and looking for sanctuary. Eastwood gives her shelter with his show, but insists that she works her passage with the rest of them, and, while the rodeo and romantic elements do not always quite jell, the movie takes on many of the aspects of some of the great comedies of the 1930s and 1940s and, in their growing on-off romance, Eastwood and Locke recall the Tracy-Hepburn style of screen confrontation.

Bronco Billy, however, received only a muted response from audiences and was, for an Eastwood picture, something of a failure. The reason for this is perhaps not too difficult to comprehend. In *Bronco Billy* Eastwood gently and charmingly guyed his macho image and audiences, who wanted him in his tough guy persona, failed to – or did not want to – share in the joke. Which was a pity since *Bronco Billy* is a warm and funny film with a performance from Eastwood that makes one note with pleasure both his range as an actor and the sheer warmth of his on-screen personality. When

I saw the movie for the second time on an aircraft flying from Los Angeles to London, *Bronco Billy* succeeded in capturing first the attention, and then the enthusiasm of a group of French schoolchildren who, up to the time the film was screened, had led several fellow passengers to contemplate taking them for a stroll along the wings. Critics may say what they like, but that kind of reception for a movie simply transcends mere critical objectivity.

Said the *New York Times*: 'Mr Eastwood, who can be as formidable behind the camera as he is in front of it, is an entertainer too', while *Now* magazine called it: '. . . a most welcome addition to the Eastwood pantheon of unconventionals. Even if the styles of the two side-by-side stories – of a rackety Wild West show and a Capra-esque heiress-on-the-run – clash too harshly for the good of the film's momentum, it has all the refreshing feel of a primitive picture painted by a sophisticate who doesn't fear emotion . . . Eastwood's way with the main events pays off in rich enjoyment. There are few enough stars around who can so mock their own image, as he does here, and yet keep it intact by the fervency of an approach that shows that beneath those satirized values are others that are just as worthwhile. That sound you hear is Clint Eastwood laughing not only at his star-myth – but at our double-take. So good-natured is the effect that we are bound to laugh along with him.' Said William Hall in the *Evening News*: 'This is the film I never thought I'd see from Eastwood, who seemed set in a mould of laconic, steely-eyed heroes that stifled him like a concrete overcoat. . . It is as if all the years of playing Spaghetti Westerns, Dirty Harry and the like, have jelled together into one concise character, fully rounded and mature – a man, at last, with a name. . . The film is funny, touching, beautifully paced, hugely entertaining. Moreover, it was directed by Eastwood himself.'

For his second outing with Clyde the orang-utan, 1980's *Any Which Way You Can*, Eastwood decided that having to deal with the amiable ape was enough, along with having to act as well, and so Buddy Van Horn directed this sequel, very much in the line of the first film *Every Which Way but Loose*. Predictably, as Eastwood and his audiences enjoyed themselves, so many critics became stuffy about it, believing no doubt that the man they had occasionally looked to as the natural heir to Don Siegel's mantle had no real business simply enjoying himself and entertaining filmgoers. Said Virginia Dignam in the *Morning Star*: 'Clint Eastwood's taciturn presence, abrasive yet self mocking, deserves better material than this mixture of violence and sentiment, ape or no ape. As Pauline Kael said in a recent article: "The queues and the box office grosses tell us only that people are going to the movies, not that they're having a good time. Film moguls think the high receipt figures are for what the audience want to see rather than what they settle for".'

One can see what Ms Kael is getting at, of course, but it also sounds like a rather acid comment by a critic who, despite all that she has to say, finds audiences going to see what they – not Ms Kael – want to see. Audiences, who, after all, have to pay for the privilege of seeing movies, are, by and large, right to ignore critics who are guides – not gods.

Eastwood has long ago proved himself to be critic-proof as far as his fans – and they

A poster for Eastwood's 1982 film *Firefox* (Warner Bros.) in which he once again returns to his role as performer of a daring and dangerous mission.

77

Far right: Eastwood in *High Plains Drifter* (Universal), presenting an appearance which, despite his 'Dirty Harry' roles, his horror and his comedies, is probably the one by which he is best known.

Right: Clint Eastwood and Sondra Locke, together with a Ronald Reagan badge. As right-wing cinema cowboys who have both been lifeguards Reagan and Eastwood have a lot in common.

are legion – are concerned, as the success of the badly mauled *Any Which Way You Can* triumphantly demonstrated. And there is a large body of critical writing to show that he is now recognized as a major actor, as well as a star and, additionally, no mean director. As he says in the guise of Bronco Billy McCoy: 'You can be anything you want. All you got to do is to get out and be it.' He chose to be a star – and an actor – and a director, and he went out and became all three, three of the best around currently. And doubtless his latest picture *Firefox* (unreleased at the time of writing) in which he is sent to steal the secrets of a vital advanced aircraft, will prove all three qualities yet again, along with his almost unerring ability to know what cinemagoers want to see at the pictures.

The last word, as is only right and proper, belongs to Eastwood himself. He has said: 'I've learned that any actor has to have something special to be a star while a lot of damned good actors are passed by. The public know they're good, but the public don't pay to see *them*, they pay to see *stars*. I didn't invent the rules. That's just the way it is.'

FILMOGRAPHY

Revenge of the Creature. 1955. Universal. Director: Jack Arnold. With John Agar, Lori Nelson, Brett Halsey, John Bromfield, Nesta Paiva.

Tarantula. 1955. Universal. Director: Jack Arnold. With Raymond Bailey, John Agar, Nestor Paiva, Leo G. Carroll.

Lady Godiva (GB: *Lady Godiva of Coventry*). 1955. Universal. Director: Arthur Lubin. With Maureen O'Hara, George Nader, Victor McLaglen.

Francis in the Navy. 1955. Universal. Director: Arthur Lubin. With Donald O'Connor, Martha Hyer, Jim Backus, David Janssen.

Never Say Goodbye. 1956. Universal. Director: Jerry Hopper. With Rock Hudson, Cornell Borchers, George Sanders, Ray Collins, David Janssen.

The First Travelling Saleslady. 1956. RKO. Director: Arthur Lubin. With Ginger Rogers, Barry Nelson, Carol Channing, Brian Keith, James Arness.

Star in the Dark. 1956. Universal. Director: Charles Haas. With John Agar, Mamie Van Doren, Richard Boone, Leif Erickson.

Escapade in Japan. 1957. RKO. Director: Arthur Lubin. With Teresa Wright, Cameron Mitchell.

Ambush at Cimarron Pass. 1957. Twentieth Century-Fox. Director: Jodie Copelan. With Scott Brady, William Vaughan, Keith Richards, Margia Dean, Irving Bacon.

Lafayette Escadrille (GB: *Hell Bent for Glory*). 1957. Warner Bros. Director: William Wellman. With Tab Hunter, Will Hutchins, Etchika Choureau, David Janssen.

Per un Pugno di Dollari (USA, GB: *For a Fistful of Dollars*). 1964. Jolly/Constantin/Ocean/United Artists. Director: Sergio Leone. With Gian Maria Volonte (John Welles), Marianne Koch, Pepe Calvo, Wolfgang Lukschy.

Per Qualche Dollari in Piu (USA, GB: *For a Few Dollars More*). 1965. Produzioni Europee Associate/Gonzales/Constantin/United Artists). Director: Sergio Leone. With Lee Van Cleef, Gian Maria Volonte, Rosemary Dexter, Klaus Klinski, Maria Krup.

Il Buono, il Brutto, il Cattivo (USA, GB: *The Good, the Bad and the Ugly*). 1966. Produzioni Europee Associate/United Artists. Director: Sergio Leone. With Eli Wallach, Lee Van Cleef.

Le Streghe (USA: *The Witches*). 1967. Dino de Laurentiis/United Artists. Directed by Vittorio de Sica. With Silvana Mangano.

Hang 'Em High. 1968. Leonard Freeman Productions/United Artists. Director: Ted Post. With Ed Begley, Pat Hingle, Inger Stevens, James MacArthur, Arlene Golonka.

Coogan's Bluff. 1968. Universal. Director: Don Siegel. With Lee J. Cobb, Susan Clark, Tisha Sterling, Don Stroud, Betty Field, Tom Tully.

Where Eagles Dare. 1969. Winkast/MGM. Director: Brian G. Hutton. With Richard Burton, Mary Ure, Patrick Wymark, Michael Hordern, Donald Houston, Anton Diffring.

Paint Your Wagon. 1969. Paramount. Director: Joshua Logan. With Lee Marvin, Jean Seberg, Harve Presnell, Ray Walston.

Two Mules for Sister Sara. 1970. Universal/Malpaso. Director: Don Siegel. With Shirley MacLaine, Manolo Fabreglas, John Kelly, Alberto Morin, Armando Silvestre.

Kelly's Heroes, 1970. MGM/Warriors/Avala. Director: Brian G. Hutton. With Telly Savalas, Don Rickles, Donald Sutherland, Carroll O'Connor.

The Beguiled. 1971. Universal/Malpaso. Director: Don Siegel. With Geraldine Page, Elizabeth Hartman, Jo Anne Harris, Mae Mercer.

Play Misty for Me. 1971. Universal/Malpaso. Director: Clint Eastwood. With Jessica Walter, Donna Mills, John Larch, Jack Ging, Irene Hervey.

Dirty Harry. 1971. Warner Bros./Malpaso. Director: Don Siegel. With Harry Guardino, Reni Santoni, Andy Robinson, John Vernon, John Larch, John Mitchum.

Joe Kidd. 1972. Universal/Malpaso. Director: John Sturges. With Robert Duvall, John Saxon, Don Stroud, Stella Garcia, James Wainwright.

High Plains Drifter. 1972. Universal/Malpaso. Director: Clint Eastwood. With Verna Bloom, Mariana Hill, Mitchell Ryan, Billy Curtis, Jack Ging.

Magnum Force. 1973. Malpaso/Columbia-Warner. Director: Ted Post. With Hal Holbrook, Felton Perry, Mitchell Ryan, David Soul, Tim Mathesen.

Thunderbolt and Lightfoot. 1974. Malpaso/United Artists. Director: Michael Cimino. With Jeff Bridges, George Kennedy, Geoffrey Lewis.

The Eiger Sanction. 1975. Universal/Malpaso. Director: Clint Eastwood. With George Kennedy, Vonetta McGee, Jack Cassidy.

The Outlaw Josey Wales. 1976. Malpaso/Warner Bros. Director: Clint Eastwood. With Chief Dan George, John Vernon, Bill McKinney, Sam Bottoms, Sondra Locke, Paula Trueman, Geraldine Kearns, Bill Sampson.

The Enforcer. 1976. Universal/Malpaso. Director: Jim Fargo. With Bradford Dillman, Harry Guardino, John Mitchum, Tyne Daly.

The Gauntlet. 1977. Universal/Malpaso. Director: Clint Eastwood. With Sondra Locke.

Every Which Way but Loose. 1977. Malpaso/Warner Bros. Director: James Fargo. With Sondra Locke, Ruth Gordon, Geoffrey Lewis, John Quade, Clyde.

Escape from Alcatraz. 1978. Paramount/Malpaso. Director: Don Siegel. With Patrick McGoohan.

Bronco Billy. 1980. Malpaso/Warner Bros. Director: Clint Eastwood. With Sondra Locke.

Any Which Way You Can. 1981. Malpaso/Warner Bros. Director: Buddy Van Horn. With Sondra Locke, Geoffrey Lewis, William Smith, Harry Guardino, Ruth Gordon, Clyde.

Firefox. 1982. Malpaso/Warner Bros. Director: Clint Eastwood.